SHOWERS OF BLESSINGS

"From Tin Roof to Talisman"

The story of Aberdeen's first suburb and its churches

by

DAVID HAGGART

Published by
Polmuir Studio
24 Polmuir Road, Aberdeen AB11 7SY
Tel: 01224 584176 Fax: 01224 582715

ISBN 0-9539388-0-8

Any profits from the sale of this book will be donated to the Ferryhill Towards 2000 fund.

Printed by Astra Print and Design

FOREWORD

THE Kirk Session of Ferryhill Parish Church invited me to write this little book. The task has been a labour of love made much easier by the cooperation I have received from many people. Posthumous credit must be given to the compilers of the Aberdeen Post Office Directory from 1870 onwards, an invaluable source of insight into the development of the city of Aberdeen and, in particular, of Ferryhill. I also needed the help of people with long memories - the star performers were undoubtedly Mary Marr and Doris Sefton who dealt patiently with my many questions. I am greatly indebted to Hazel Braynion for undertaking to liaise with our printers and to negotiate (very successfully) with the copyright owners of the photographs which appear in the book. In this connection special thanks are due to to Eric Stevenson (Aberdeen Journals), Mike Dey (Aberdeen Art Gallery), Catherine Taylor (Aberdeen City Library), Winram's Bookshop and Mike Craig (University of Aberdeen Queen Mother Library). I must also thank Shelagh and James Bain who, along with Fred Coutts, made some last-minute photographic illustrations possible. I am also grateful to Neil Garden of Astra Print & Design for taking a personal interest in the project and guiding us through the complexities of design and production. Publication of the book was made possible by a group of "angels" who generously underwrote the costs. Finally my thanks go to Hazel Braynion, Ian Dick and Lorna Glen for reading drafts and spotting errors, and, above all, to my wife Gwen, proof-reader *extraordinaire*.

David Haggart

I will cause my people and their homes around my holy hill to be a blessing. And I will send showers, showers of blessings, which will come just when they are needed.

Ezekiel 34:26

The "Iron Kirk" which served as the first Ferryhill Parish Church. It is pictured here after being re-located at Ruthrieston.

IN THE BEGINNING - 1870

IN 1870 there were no churches in Ferryhill. By 1874 there were two, built within nine months of each other, forming part of a remarkable church extension programme in Aberdeen which transformed the city spiritually, socially and architecturally. These were exciting times. Middle aged Aberdonians had seen many changes. The railway was no longer a novelty, but it had only reached Aberdeen (to be precise, Ferryhill) in 1850. The Joint Station was five years old and the Tay Bridge was still under construction. The telephone was not to arrive for some years, but the Society of Telegraph Engineers was established in 1871, giving respectability to a technology that had brought about a revolution in communications. The people of Aberdeen were no longer isolated from the rest of the world. They knew what was going on thanks to the six newspapers published in the city, particularly the daily Aberdeen Free Press and the Aberdeen Journal, published every Wednesday. In their closely printed columns had come news of the American Civil War, followed by details of the Impeachment of President Andrew Johnson - to remain a unique event until 1999. As the Ferryhill kirks were being built, the President was the famous Civil War general, Ulysses P Grant. European news included the death of Napoleon III. From India came details of the assassination of the Viceroy, Lord Mayo. In Britain the reins of government were in the hands of Mr Gladstone, who had defeated Disraeli in 1868. His cabinet did not include a Secretary for Scotland - that office was not created until 1885. Aberdeen was represented in Parliament by a Liberal, John Farley Leith. He was an English barrister who on one occasion took the chair at the AGM of Bon Accord Swimming Club. He was by no means renowned as an orator, but on that occasion it is reported that he brought the house down by reciting the Shakespearean passage in which Cassius recalls how his swimming prowess saved the life of Julius Caesar. Local affairs were in the hands of a Town Council presided over by Lord Provost William Leslie, an architect who must have taken a close professional interest not only in the explosion of church building that was in progress, but in the planning and lay out of the new streets required to accommodate the rapid expansion of the city. A lot was going on. On Sunday afternoon walks the citizens could inspect the progress being made in the construction of the new Free Church tower in Rotunda

Place (no Fonthill Road yet) or turn north to enjoy the amenities of the brand new Victoria Park, the city's first. It would be another ten years before they could take the air in the Duthie Park, but a pleasant walk to Torry was possible, thanks to the Wellington Suspension Bridge, built in 1830 to replace the ferry which, from ancient times, had given the area its name.

Aberdeen was expanding in all possible directions. The catalyst for this had been, of course, the inspired civil engineering work which led to the creation of Union Street. From this came important arteries to north, west and south - King Street, George Street, Union Terrace (followed by Rosemount Viaduct in 1883), Albyn Place, Holburn Street, Market Street

Taken around 1890 by the George Washington Wilson Company, this view from Craiginches shows the Ferryhill Foundry on the extreme left.

A George Washington Wilson photograph taken from Kincorth around 1885. On the far left, Arthurseat House marks the position of the Duthie Park tennis courts. Polmuir House can be seen in the centre of the picture, near the railway arches.

and Crown Street. It was the latter, along with the arrival of the railway, that provided the life blood for Ferryhill.

At the beginning of the 19th century the centre of Aberdeen was in a transitional phase. Union Street had been built, but most of its "tributary" streets had yet to be fully developed and the Green still retained some of the characteristics of the city centre which had been its role for centuries. So it was from the Green, via a bridge over the Denburn (now inside the Trinity Centre Car Park) and Windmill Brae that you reached the Hardgate, main road to the south west. There was also a branch road to the south across lands owned by Marischal College, hence the name College Street. The extension which we know as South College Street was called Wellington Road. This was the old route to Ferryhill. Along that axis there was some early industrial development. From a much earlier period bricks had been made using the natural resource of the Clayhills close to Dee Village (which disappeared when the electricity station was constructed at the foot of Crown Street). Now in that same area, the popular building material of the 19th century was processed at Petrie's Granite Works. Not far away, near the Suspension Bridge was Abernethy's iron foundry and a little further south the Devanha Brewery. In the middle of the century the railway arrived. At first it reached only as far as Ferryhill Station which was built close to the north end of the new railway bridge. Later the line was extended to the Joint Station. The industrial sector was, therefore, confined to a narrow ribbon from College Street to the railway arches. The rest of what we now know as Ferryhill was a residential area based on Crown Street and, to a lesser extent, Bon Accord Street along with the various thoroughfares that connected them laterally. The upper part of Crown Street included the houses of professional people - doctors and ministers among them. There were a few commercial premises including those of the distinguished photographer George Washington Wilson. Further down the street flats in the handsome tenements were occupied by all sorts of artisans and craftsmen including many linked to the shipping industry and the railway which was now a major employer. One of Aberdeen's most

Crown Street - a quiet residential street, seen here before the building of the Post Office.

Dee Village in 1898 looking from Millburn Street towards Crown Street. Next year it was demolished to make way for the electricity station.

famous sea-faring characters, Captain William Penny, was in residence at 1 South Crown Street. Bon Accord Square consisted entirely of private residences - with occupiers including advocates, professors and ministers. Bon Accord Street, which terminated at Springbank Terrace (no bridge built yet), boasted a more varied population. Residents included the ever present ministers, a professor of music, shipmasters, surgeons and, perhaps most interesting of all, W. Robb bird-stuffer. Ferryhill Place and Marine Place were fully occupied, but only two residents are listed in Marine Terrace. Building had begun in Albury Road and the occupant of No 1 was Duncan McMillan who, at the time of our historical snapshot, must have been spending much of his time with the builders in Rotunda Place - he was the architect of the new Free Church and was to be its Session Clerk for many years.

FERRYHILL

THE pattern of early 19th Century Ferryhill was of terraced houses and tenements coming down Bon Accord Street to Springbank, and down Crown Street to South Crown Street, Ferryhill Place, Abbotsford Place, Devanha Terrace and Prospect Terrace. This was the built-up part. Everywhere else there were suburban mansions standing in large gardens. Some of the houses still stand, although they are now cheek by jowl with the modern houses built in their gardens. Gardens were an important feature in Ferryhill. The Directory of the time records the name of the owner of each property and the name of the gardener. The houses included Ferryhill House (today's hotel), Old Ferryhill House (off Prospect Terrace), Devanha House, Deemount, Polmuir (near the railway viaduct), Arthurseat (near the Duthie Park tennis courts), Maryfield, East Bank and West Bank. Another prominent building was the Oldmachar Poorhouse, later to become the Prince Charles Barracks. Although "big hooses" with large gardens made up much of the Ferryhill landscape, the dominant feature that would strike the eye of anyone standing at the view point now occupied by Ferryhill Parish Church would be Roy's Nurseries. John Roy was in a big way of business. He had a shop at 48 Union Street, but his major concerns were the nurseries and market gardens which appear to have covered the whole area from Fonthill Road almost to the railway. The nursery ground was feud out from the 1870's onward and it was on this land that Polmuir Road, Sycamore Place, Brunswick Place, Bright Street and Murray Terrace were built. In 1873 there may have been a few cottages on the site, but the only substantial house was Rotunda Lodge. The name "Rotunda" was also applied to the east end of what is now Fonthill Road and to the top of Polmuir Road. "Rotunda" is believed to be a reference to the "Round O", a geological feature that could be seen until a few years ago in the grounds of the Cowdray Club. Some writers assign the "Round O" name to a deep chasm in the grounds of 14 Polmuir Road that is also known as the Ferryhill Kettlehole. In 1872 Duncan McMillan was able to secure an area of ground at the North East corner of Roy's Nurseries as the site for a new Free Church.

According to solicitors and estate agencies one of the attractions of Ferryhill in 2000 is its proximity to the city centre, but in the early 1870s

They look as if they are bound for a funeral, but these employees of Devanha Brewery are in fact setting off for their annual outing.

the area was being developed as Aberdeen's first suburb. Rosemount, Rubislaw and Mannofield were soon to follow, but it was Ferryhill which first offered an escape from the narrow, cluttered streets that originated in the mediaeval town, and covered not much more than a square mile around the Castlegate. Change would come rapidly. Torry had already come within the city bounds, but Old Aberdeen was still a separate burgh. The union of King's College and Marischal College to form the University was still something of a novelty as was the Free Kirk College in Alford Place. The Music

Hall had already become a familiar landmark in Union Street, but the Town House was only completed in 1874. The Scotch Education Act was passed in 1872 and would lead to universal schooling, but until that happened there was complex and varied provision in the city. The School Board was responsible for 6 fairly large establishments including the Grammar School. Churches of various denominations ran 19 schools, and there were no fewer than 30 other day and boarding schools, mostly run as private enterprises, but including some owned by charities. In a category of its own was Gordon's Hospital, later to be known as Robert Gordon's College. The demand for education and information was further demonstrated by the proliferation of lending libraries. Milne's Select Library and Reading Club at 201 Union Street allowed you to borrow up to 16 books at a time for an annual subscription of 5 guineas. According to the Board of Trade, a labourer's weekly wage in 1872 was 11 shillings and 9 pence, so the library subscription probably represented the amount that today's working man or woman would spend on running a car for a year. Ferryhill was obviously a very convenient place to live for those who wanted to make use of railway connections that were still developing rapidly. It was also handy for the harbour where you could board a steamship for Newcastle, occupying a first class cabin for 12 shillings. The residents of Ferryhill were also within comfortable walking distance of the brand new His Majesty's Opera House which opened in December 1872. On its stage Aberdonians would in the next 30 years see many wonderful shows including performances by the original D'Oyly Carte Company and personal appearances by Sir Henry Irving, Beerbohm Tree and Ellen Terry. It became the Tivoli in 1910, and, although for the moment only ghostly artistes tread its boards, it's still there.

THE DISRUPTION

IF you are over 45 you can probably remember what was happening 30 years ago and it will not seem very distant. That would apply to every one living in Scotland in the early 1870s in relation to the Disruption. This was a major event in Scottish church history. In 1843 the Kirk split in two on the question of patronage - the right of lairds and landowners to influence the choice of parish ministers. Overnight a new denomination was created. In Aberdeen the division was total. Every minister "came out" of the Established Church and set up a congregation of the Free Church. There was much enthusiasm for the new denomination and in cities like Aberdeen many of the well-to-do business people were attracted to it. With income tax at 3 pence in the pound, the wealthy shipowners and merchants of Aberdeen had cash available to fund church building at an astonishing rate. In the case of St Clement's Church in Footdee, the speed was mind boggling. Between 18th May, when their minister "came out" at the Disruption Assembly in Edinburgh and 4th June, the first Sunday after he returned to Aberdeen, the congregation had secured a site and erected a church! By 1873, the Established Church with 9 parishes had been totally outstripped by the Free Church with 18, not to mention the 6 United Presbyterian congregations. Add to that, 6 Congregational, 3 Evangelical Union, 6 Episcopal, 2 Methodist, 3 Baptist, 2 Roman Catholic, at least 2 Brethren meetings and 1 each of Associate Synod, Quakers, Unitarians and Glassites and you can see why so many houses were occupied by ministers!

If Irving Berlin had written "Anything you can do I can do better" in 1870 instead of in the 1940s, it could have been sung very appropriately at most meetings of the Established and Free Church Presbyteries. In the aftermath of the 1843 Disruption, new Free Church buildings sprang up in every parish, and as the city began to expand, the two denominations stalked each other round the developing areas seeking the best sites and vying for the services of the best architects. How much of this was done consciously, it is hard to say, but the evidence of competition is there to be seen in granite throughout the city as splendid churches (some now disused) face each other across the street or, in the case of Ferryhill, at top and bottom of a hill.

TWO KIRKS ARE BETTER THAN ONE

IF there was a race, it began when the idea occurred to someone in either the Established Church or the Free Church that the denomination should be represented in Ferryhill. The next step would be for that individual to take his (only men in those days) idea to a Presbytery. This happened in Aberdeen Free Presbytery in May 1872 and was followed by a meeting in November of that year when it was resolved to form a congregation in Ferryhill and build a church. Building started in May 1873 and was due to last a year. Meanwhile the Established Church, through the Aberdeen Church Extension Association, had also decided to build in Ferryhill. Maybe they took the decision earlier than the Free Church, or perhaps they felt the need to catch up with their rivals (the use of this word does seem to be justified). They decided to accelerate matters. The construction of a proper granite building was postponed. Instead they erected a corrugated iron temporary church at the junction of Caledonian Lane and Ferryhill Road. This was opened for worship as a Chapel of Ease in October 1873, while the Free Church at the top of the hill was still only half-built. Members of both denominations were given a spiritual boost when it was announced that the famous American evangelists Moody and Sankey were to include Aberdeen in their British tour. They drew immense audiences, but according to popular report, Dwight Moody was a "heavy laborious speaker" and it was Ira Sankey who pleased the crowds with his sentimental hymns and choruses.

The Established Church, having won the building race in Ferryhill, also gained a gifted minister to see them through their early years. The Revd Henry Cowan, minister of the West (St Nicholas) Church was an enthusiast for church extension, and resigned his charge in 1873 with the intention of becoming the first minister of the new Rubislaw Church. This may have been a premature decision, because the Rubislaw church was not completed until 1875, so when the iron kirk at Ferryhill became available, Mr Cowan offered his services. In due course he left for Rubislaw, but not before he had got things off to a very good start at Ferryhill. He was regarded as an eloquent and inspiring preacher and went on to become Professor of Church History at Aberdeen University. He was succeeded in 1875 by the Revd Henry Wright, first minister to be ordained and inducted to Ferryhill Parish Church. By this time a decision had been taken to build a proper stone and lime church on the site. In due course the iron church building was dismantled and re-erected near the bridge over the Ruthrieston burn (today Riverside Place is adjacent) to serve as the first spiritual home for the congregation that would eventually occupy Ruthrieston South Church. The "Iron Kirkie" was subsequently transported to Fyvie where, sadly, a destructive outbreak of fire ended its peregrinations.

The fact that the site at the top of the hill was made available for the Free Church was one of several indications that Roy's Nurseries were being feud out and put up for sale. More residences would be built on the southern slope, so the strategic position of the site for a parish church was further enhanced. The leading lights at the public meeting held in November 1872 had been Principal Lumsden of the Free Church College and Mr William Henderson of Devanha. They secured the services of Duncan McMillan as architect. William Henderson, who was to be a generous benefactor to the church for many years, later became Lord Provost of Aberdeen and was knighted by Queen Victoria. How he found time to be a successful business man would be mystifying if we did not know that he married the daughter of his boss and so became head of a major shipping company. Apart from being a councillor and elected member of the School Board, he was an office-bearer of the British and Foreign Bible Society, the National Bible Society of Scotland, Aberdeen Reformation Society, Aberdeen YMCA, the Aberdeen Auxiliary of the London Missionary Society, Aberdeen Evangelical Association, the University Missionary Union and the China Mission Committee. There were probably more, those just happen to be organisations listed in the Aberdeen Directory. Perhaps it was Henderson's interest in foreign missions that led to a famous Indian missionary, Dr Duff, being invited to preach at the opening service on Sunday 28th June 1874. There were three services on that day. Dr Duff preached in the morning, Principal Lumsden in the evening. The afternoon service was taken by the man who had accepted a call to become the fledgling congregation's first minister, the Revd James Iverach.

THE DAYS OF WRIGHT AND IVERACH

HENRY Wright, having arrived at Ferryhill Parish Church only a few months before the "Iron Kirkie" was dismantled in 1875, stayed for the rest of his life - there would be no work for a vacancy committee until 1924. Up the hill, several ministers came and went during that period, but James Iverach never went away. In 1887 he became a Professor at the Free Church College in Alford Place, but he continued to reside in Ferryhill Place and remained a member of Ferryhill Free

Church (and of its Kirk Session) until his death in 1922. For almost half a century these two men, Wright and Iverach, dominated the church scene in Ferryhill - arriving as bright young men, earning the love and respect of their people over many years, and eventually achieving the status of patriarchs. Elsewhere significant personalities included Gladstone and Disraeli, Orville and Wilbur Wright, Dan Leno and Marie Lloyd, Lenin and Trotsky, Asquith and Lloyd George - but in Ferryhill the names to conjure with were Henry Wright and James Iverach.

Those who accompanied the two ministers on their Pilgrimages in Ferryhill lived through a lot of history. The wonderful new railway bridge over the Tay collapsed in a storm in 1879. The first practicable electric lights were produced in 1882. Marconi sent a wireless message to someone over a mile away in 1895. In the same year Rontgen invented X Rays and Freud introduced the world to psycho-analysis. Then there was the Boer War, the San Francisco earthquake, the invention of the aeroplane and the motor car, the introduction of Old Age Pensions, the sinking of the Titanic, the First World War, the Russian Revolution. Through it all James Iverach lived at 12 Ferryhill Place; Henry Wright flitted once - from 34 Ferryhill Place to 26 Polmuir Road.

STONE AND LIME

IF the sight of a fine new Free Kirk, costing £5,500, at the top of the hill served as a spur to the folk of the Parish Church, so too did the celebrated philanthropist James Baird. He responded to an appeal from the City of Aberdeen Church Extension Association by offering the sum of £7,500 to assist in the building and endowment of five churches. A century and a quarter later this may seem to be a drop in the bucket, but remember the labourer's weekly wage of 11/9d. The Association immediately accepted the munificent donation and the conditions which accompanied it which included a stipulation that the churches be built of stone and within a specified time. Thus the days of the "Iron Kirkie" at Ferryhill were numbered. William Smith, the City Architect, drew up plans for a stone church to seat 800 worshippers. It was to cost £3,858 and the newly arrived minister, Henry Wright, found himself thrown into the business of fund-raising. Bazaars, courses of lectures and generous donations from individuals and organisations soon provided the necessary wherewithal to enable building work to commence. It must have been obvious to everyone that the new building, while commodious and elegantly designed, would scarcely match the grandeur of the Free Church with its impressive tower and commanding situation. However, during the construction work, Henry Wright came up with an idea which must have cheered the hearts of any of his friends in whose secret hearts the competitive spirit stirred. He proposed that an organ should be installed in the new church. Not totally earth shattering, perhaps, but at that time instrumental music of any kind was rare in Scottish churches. In Aberdeen, St Clement's Parish Church installed an organ in 1875. That was the first. Ferryhill would be second, but not until a special congregational meeting unanimously agreed that this very progressive step should be taken. Whether anyone mentioned that the Free Church was still dependent on a precentor to lead the praise, is not noted. Dr Peace of Glasgow Cathedral was consulted and an organ was purchased from Conachers of Huddersfield at a cost of £430. It was installed in May 1877, three months before the new church opened for public worship. By 1922, not surprisingly, the organ was in need of some serious (and expensive) attention. A debt was incurred. To defray this the organist of Oldmachar Cathedral was invited to give a recital - admission one shilling. In December 1879 Ferryhill Chapel was raised to full status - becoming a Quoad Sacra Parish Church - and on 18th January 1880 the ordination of 8 elders took place. Andrew Collie was appointed Session Clerk. He lived at 1 Caledonian Place within easy walking distance of his grocer's shop in Union Street - destined to receive the royal warrant and become the Fortnum and Mason of Aberdeen. Andrew Collie's neighbours in Caledonian Place included Captain Charles Watson and his wife Elizabeth. In 1903, Captain Watson, by then a widower, died and bequeathed the sum of £100 to the church to provide an ornamental glass window in memory of his wife. Four Aberdeen glaziers were invited to submit designs, the successful firm being Messrs Gordon and Watt. The new window, depicting a Nativity scene from which Joseph appears to have been excused, was in place in the south transept by October 1904. Just over 90 years later the window was re-installed as the main feature of the apse in the present Ferryhill Parish Church.

MUSIC

IT is possible, in fact quite likely, that Henry Wright was himself an organist. Tributes paid to him at various times refer to his musical abilities and "fine musical tastes". William Carnie, the celebrated journalist, called him "the most accomplished minister musician Aberdeen ever had". He was president of the Wagner Society and gave lectures on Handel, Haydn, Mozart and Beethoven. The opportunities, in the early part of his ministry, for him or anyone else in Aberdeen to hear the music of any of these composers must have been limited to chamber music performances and concerts by the Aberdeen Choral Union. Regular visits by professional symphony orchestras were still some distance off, and it is hard to conceive of any Wagnerian operas being staged in Aberdeen before the opening of His Majesty's Theatre in 1906. However, a few years after the Wrights moved into their new manse, the gramophone came on the scene, bringing music to the farthest corners of the globe and, you may be certain, to 26 Polmuir Road. In 1913 the University of Aberdeen made Henry Wright a Doctor of Divinity "in recognition of his pastoral work and zeal in the promotion of musical culture in the city and district". He also promoted it assiduously in his own church. Details of music to be used in worship were published in advance in the church magazine. At each service (morning and evening) there would be an anthem, and a chanted prose psalm plus one or two hymns. It was the practice of the time for the congregation to stand during the anthems, some of which were quite lengthy. This may have been the cause of one of the few ripples to disturb the tranquillity of kirk session meetings at this era. In 1919 an elder asked if the possibility of sitting for anthems could be discussed. He was answered in the negative, with the information that the session had "no locus" in this matter which was entirely in the minister's province. A month later the same elder tried again. This time, while ruling the matter ultra vires as far as the session was concerned, Dr Wright indicated that he would use his prerogative (and the Wisdom of Solomon) to resolve matters. The next issue of the church bulletin intimates that "in deference to a feeling believed to prevail among a majority of the members of the church, the congregation will be requested to remain seated during the singing of the anthem". During this period there was also a flourishing Sunday School Choir which occasionally contributed to morning worship as well as giving performances of operettas and sacred cantatas.

From the earliest days the Parish Church Magazine was a simple four page document, and that format was retained for seventy years. In the 1880's the fourth page usually carried advertising, doubtless providing some income to cover publication costs. The December 1883 issue included an announcement from Messrs T.R. Watson's funeral establishment to the effect that telephonic communication had been established with their Ferryhill agent, Mr George Angus. This gentleman was the founder of a grocer's business in Bank Street, destined to remain in business for over a hundred years. Thus, it appears that a representative of a bereaved family had only to call at the grocer's to summon the undertaker.

LITERARY DELIGHTS

AT this time the magazine also contained several poetic contributions from Janet Miller. She may have been a member of the congregation, possibly one of the two Miss Millers who lived at 158 Crown Street and sat, just below the pulpit, in Pew No 10. Her gift for simple expression can be seen in the following lines from "A Summer Day on the Kincardineshire Coast":

The golden glow of summer eve,
When nature sinks to dewy rest;
The murmur of the gentle breeze,
The swallow hastening to her nest;
Each sight and sound to eye and ear
Proclaim the goodness of Thy love;
And we would join our praises here
To nobler anthems sung above.

The University focussed on Henry Wright's efforts to promote interest in music, but he also laboured hard to help his congregation to appreciate the delights of English literature. In 1902 he formed the Reading Union which continued to meet in the manse every month for the remainder of his ministry. The idea was simple. At the start of each session Dr Wright would produce a reading list, and at the monthly meetings he would explain, elucidate and encourage discussion. By 1906 the list of works the group had read and studied was beginning to look quite awesome: two books by Carlyle - *Heroes and Hero-Worship* and *The French Revolution*; Tennyson's *In Memoriam;* Scott's *Waverley*, *The Antiquary*, *Guy Mannering*, and *Lady of the Lake*; Forster's *Life of Goldsmith*; Lamb's *Essays of Elia*; Shakespeare's *Richard III*, *As You Like It*, *Merchant of Venice*, *The Tempest*, *Julius Caesar* and *Twelfth Night*. It went on like that for over 20 years, providing a literary education of quite extraordinary breadth. In May 1913, not long after he received his doctorate, Dr Wright was presented with a framed address signed by 20 members of the Readers' Union. It included these words: "As we grow older, we find it increasingly difficult to lift ourselves out of the groove of daily life, but the meetings of the Readers' Union are occasions when we rise above petty troubles, and spend a peaceful hour in a literary atmosphere." The appeal of literature was perhaps not universal in the congregation. Guild Notes for January 1922 record that the Rev A Austin Foster was not favoured with a large audience when he gave an excellent lecture on Browning's *Cleon*. The next speaker on the syllabus was to be the scientist Dr John Boyd Orr, destined for international celebrity status. The Guild was founded early in the history of the parish as an organisation for young men and women. It flourished for a while, then withered. In 1913 it revived and appears to have enjoyed a lively existence until the outbreak of the Second World War - educational topics always being prominent in its programme. From 1926 the Guild ran in parallel with the branch of the Woman's Guild which was formed at a special meeting of the "women workers" of the congregation.

AN ERA CLOSES

IN March 1914 Dr Wright reviewed the state of the congregation to which he had been ministering for 38 years. Membership had grown to 1065, there were 33 elders and 9 managers. The Sunday School roll stood at 335, but the Bible Class had only 25 in attendance and, according to Dr Wright, was short of "lads". The latter were more numerous at the

Revd Dr Henry Wright, first minister of Ferryhill Parish Church.

Boys' Brigade which had a membership of 60. The revived Guild had attracted 63 members and 30 members of the Ladies' Work Party were responsible for delivering 420 copies of "Life and Work" each month.

By the time of Dr Wright's death just before Christmas 1923, the roll of the Parish Church was approaching 1400. For 45 years of his ministry he had visited every member once a year. His love of the congregation was reflected in the terms of his will in which he bequeathed the residue of his estate to the church. At his memorial service the Interim Moderator said of him, ".... Dr Wright was above all a good man. Though his modest and retiring disposition constrained him to shun publicity and active participation in work beyond the bounds of his own church and congregation, his winsome personality laid its spell on all who came in contact with him, however casually." This had certainly proved to be the case in his relations with the people of Ferryhill Free Church (which became United Free in 1899). It was the UF minister, David Mair, who wrote the obituary notice for the Press and Journal.

Since 1917 the two congregations had become accustomed to worshipping together at holiday times and their various organisations shared many joint events. As well they might, because Patronage, the issue at the root of the Disruption, had been abolished in 1875 - removing the only compelling reason for having two separate denominations. There were other differences, mainly relating to church government. A century later they seem comparatively trivial, but they were enough to keep the two sides apart for another 50 years. During Dr Wright's time at Ferryhill, the Established Church's building programme saw the creation of new parishes at Rubislaw, Trinity, Rosemount, St George's in the West, Mannofield, Craigiebuckler, and Ruthrieston (South). The Free Church, already well in the lead as we have seen, responded with Causewayend, Queen's Cross and Ruthrieston (West). Apart from the sandstone eccentricity of Rubislaw, the granite architectural heritage of Aberdeen was thus created - the aesthetic consequence of a chronic ecclesiastical disagreement between churchmen whose successors would in due course have to cope with the economic consequences. Ironically, while the spires of Free and Established Kirks vied with each other at many street corners, it was General Booth who secured the best site and possibly the most exciting architecture - the Aberdeen Citadel, built at a cost of £23,000, was opened in June 1896.

THE CITY DEVELOPS

THE period when Messrs Wright and Iverach were kenspeckle figures in Ferryhill saw many more changes taking place in Aberdeen. Within stones' throws of each other, the Art Gallery, Public Library, Central School and His Majesty's Theatre all appeared, and the construction of the Cowdray Hall was just beginning. The tramway system, which had begun (horse-drawn) in 1872, was electrified between 1899 and 1902 and the line to Ferryhill, running along Fonthill Road, was opened in 1903. In September 1896 the organist of Rubislaw Church, Burwood Nicholls was invited to play the piano in the Music Hall for a presentation of Animated Photographs. The cinema had arrived in Aberdeen. Over the next few years, cinematograph exhibitions were given in many halls, often as part of a variety concert. This preceded a phase of cinema building that rivalled the efforts of the Free Kirk after the Disruption - in quantity if not quality, though quality was not always entirely absent. The Gaiety opened in 1908 on the site in the Shiprow that would eventually be occupied by the ABC Cinema. Next came the Picturedrome in 1910 - the original building still stands in Skene Terrace. The signs now say Forum and Stage Door Restaurant but to the older generation it is the Cinema House. By the end of the Wright/Iverach era the people of Ferryhill could choose from at least 13 venues showing silent movies. More were to come until by 1939 (and 10 years of talkies) Aberdeen's 19 picture palaces led to the claim that the city had the highest ratio of cinemas per head of population in Scotland. The fact that Dundee, with only a slightly higher population, had 22 cinemas might be said to weaken the claim. The fact remains that in the 1870s people competed to build bigger and better churches, but in the 1920s it was the Cinema that kept the architects busy. In a few cases 19th century churches were transformed to become 20th century picture houses. You can still see the Globe, formerly Nelson Street UP Church and now a commercial warehouse, and the Lyceum, once John Street Evangelical Union Church, later to be a Salvation Army centre and now the Cafe Grande.

PROGRESS AND TRAGEDY IN FERRYHILL

DURING the half century in which Henry Wright was spreading spiritual and cultural enlightenment from his base at the foot of the hill, there were many comings and goings and lots of things happening up at the Free Church. Indeed, a lot happened in Ferryhill generally. Polmuir Road was completed, more or less as it is today until you turn the corner at the Duthie Park. The Park itself deserves more detailed attention, but at this point we can mention that its creation involved the disappearance of the original Sycamore Place which ran from the foot of

Polmuir Road to a point just past the site of the Winter Gardens. Murray Terrace was laid out and built, leaving space on the south side for a railway station that was never built - the houses that were eventually put there are quite different in style from the older terraced villas. The new Sycamore Place would have to wait until the thirties, but the feuing out of Roy's Nurseries continued with the creation of Brunswick Place and Bright Street. The original plan for the latter was that it would continue northwards and swing round to join Polmuir Road - it never happened but the grassy lane next to 22 Polmuir Road shows where the junction would have been. The gardens of Devanha House retained their name but were turned into streets.

A London newspaper's illustration of the Dee Ferry-boat Disaster in 1876. The kilts and plaids reflect a southern image of Aberdonians.

Over-development was avoided (for the time being) by leaving space for the Four Courts Tennis Club just opposite Devanha House and the Ferryhill Bowling and Tennis Club round the corner in Polmuir Road, of which the bowling green still survives. A beginning was made to develop the grounds of Deemount House, although most of the building there came later. Fonthill Road was completed and the construction of a bridge at Springbank Terrace allowed Bon Accord Street to extend southwards. The gardens of Ferryhill House were still intact, but not for long. Possibly the most important development came just a couple of years after the churches opened - the building of Ferryhill School which admitted its first pupils in 1877.

It is doubtful if the wider world paid any attention to the building of two churches and a school, but a location not far from Ferryhill did hit the headlines of the London newspapers in 1876, even meriting an illustration in "Police News". The event which brought this attention was a tragedy that must have affected the whole community, not least the ministers and members of the two new churches. Wednesday 5th April was the Sacramental Fast, a public holiday. The weather was bright and spring-like, ideal for an inexpensive day out to Torry, taking the ferry which plied from Point Law (today Ferry Place on Provost Mearns Quay marks the spot) to a destination, only 160 yards away on the Torry quayside. However, the very mildness of the weather had brought about a rapid thawing of snow in upper Deeside. The water was exceptionally high and there was a rapid current. As the crowds of passengers increased, the boatmen became anxious. The ferry boat was new and substantially built. It was operated by a wire rope fixed to each bank, passing along the length of the boat and cranked by a wheel in the middle of the vessel. Shortly after 3 o'clock in the afternoon the boat left the Aberdeen side with 76 passengers - far too many. Their weight brought the edge of the boat to within an inch or two of the water. Half way across it was caught by the current and carried down stream so that the rope became taut. Instead of a straight line across the river there was now a triangle with the boat at its apex. It was impossible to crank the wheel. They were stuck, the boat was canting to the west and water was flowing in. There were a number of small boats in the river at the time and others pulled up on the banks. Everyone could have been rescued. But there was panic. It seemed a good idea to try to release the boat which was now immobile and likely to sink in the middle of the river. This was a tragic misunderstanding of the situation. The wire rope was cut at the Torry side, giving such momentum to the boat that it turned over completely throwing all the passengers into the water. Boats were immediately launched from both sides of the river, but although many heroic rescues took place, 32 of the passengers were drowned, mostly young men in their teens and twenties. The report of the enquiry which followed the disaster gave a fillip to plans to construct a bridge over the Dee, and from 1881 Torry was linked to Aberdeen by the Victoria Bridge. Incidentally, the illustration of the disaster in "Police News" was an artist's impression in which most of the people are depicted in kilts and tartan - a clue as to how Aberdonians were perceived in the south.

A PARK IS BORN

THE name "Ferryhill" is a very old one. The cot-toun of Ferryhill appears in some of the earliest maps of Aberdeen. People would understand the name because they knew about the ferry that crossed the Dee from the foot of the "Monkey Brae" to Craiglug. In the present century strangers trying to locate Ferryhill are told that it is close to the Duthie Park. The opening of the park in 1883 must have been a hugely significant event for the members of the two kirks which were still in their first decade. Until 1870 the only place available to the citizens of Aberdeen for outdoor recreation was the Links. Then an affluent Town Council created the Victoria Park on grazing fields known as Glennie's Parks. It proved very popular and the Council began to consider claims of the central and south-western parts of the city for similar consideration. The idea of Union Terrace Gardens was born and other sites near Union Grove and Carden Place were proposed. Then the Council grasped an opportunity to buy a strip of land lying between Allenvale Cemetery and the grounds of Arthurseat which stood nearer the railway. The hope was that if Arthurseat came on the market, the Council could add its lands to the Allenvale strip and create a public park. Unfortunately, at that point the affluence of the Town Council changed overnight to virtual penury when they lost a law-suit to the University. The park project was aborted, but not forgotten. Then Miss Elizabeth Crombie Duthie, whose family had for two generations owned the lands of Ruthrieston came into big money. She inherited estates of her uncle and brother, both wealthy lawyers. To quote her own words: "There having fallen to my lot, in the providence of God, much larger means than are needed for my own wants, I considered how I could devote a portion of my abundance for the good of the City of Aberdeen." She consulted Lord Provost George Jamieson who had a Good Idea. Within a short time Miss Duthie had purchased the Allenvale strip from the Council, added some more of the cemetery company's land and offered to buy Arthurseat, turn the whole lot into a park and present it to the city. The only problem was that Arthurseat was in the hands of a factor who had no authority to sell it, the true owner having disappeared in Australia 20 years previously. Parliamentary action was required to effect a compulsory purchase. This was achieved by the Aberdeen Corporation Act of 1881 and in August of that year the ceremony of Cutting the First Turf was performed by the Earl of

The royal procession crosses Union Bridge on its way to the opening of the Duthie Park in 1883.

The great and the good attended the opening of the Duthie Park. Fortunately most of them took their umbrellas.

Another view of the Duthie Park opening ceremony - the rain appears to have eased off.

Aberdeen in front of a decorated grandstand seating 300 leading citizens (all male) while nearly 10,000 more humble Aberdonians looked on. The latter probably got wet because "the weather unfortunately was none of the best." At the banquet which followed (cake, wine and fruit) a poetic tribute to Miss Duthie was recited. It included the lines:

Today, first foot upon the green sward,
Hastening to give a gracious welcome
The Lady comes, to make unto the City
Her noble gift.
While all around, the many-voiced throng,
The countless thousands,
One in heart and thought,
Whispering perpetual thanks,
Burst into song, which rising
Over tent and tower and tree,
Is hymned to measured cadence
By the murmurs of the Dee.

This was followed by the toast of "Bon Accord" and three hearty cheers. Two years later, landscaping and construction having been completed expeditiously, most of the company and many other distinguished guests were back for the official opening of the park. This was a really grand event. Queen Victoria couldn't come, but she sent Princess Beatrice to open a bazaar for the Sick Children's Hospital in the morning, have lunch in the Imperial Hotel, and declare the Duthie Park open in the afternoon. A similar visit by the Prince of Wales or the Princess Royal today would probably earn no more than three minutes coverage on the local television news. But in 1883, royal visits were rare and the town went gyte. Every part of the city that the Princess would pass through was decorated, almost to the point of obliteration. In Crown Street "gaily decorated stands for the use of spectators occupied positions of vantage along the street - the largest being one which successfully covered what would have been the only eyesore on the route, the dilapidated remains of Dee Village". Venetian masts were introduced to enhance the beauty of Ferryhill Place. A floral arch in the Gothic style was erected over Whinhill Road at its junction with Fonthill

The West gate of the Duthie Park decorated for the official opening by Princess Beatrice in 1883.

Road. A temporary railway station was built at the north-west corner of the park to save the Princess the necessity of getting into her coach again to travel half a mile. Pavilions, marquees and grandstands were erected in the park. There were 27 carriages and a foot procession comprising 5 marching bands and over 3000 tradesmen (with banners) and representatives of corporate bodies all under the command of Sergeant-Major Middleton of the Gordon Highlanders. Unfortunately it rained. Everybody was agreed that the weather was better than it had been the day before. But it rained. The official account reports: "Just as the Choral Union began the singing of the The Hallelujah Chorus, small raindrops gave place to large ones, and throughout the rest of the ceremony these kept pouring pitilessly down, necessitating the display of a perfect forest of umbrellas." Such shelter would not be available to the marching men - their spirits were kept up by the cheers of the onlookers and the bells of St Mary's Cathedral which "rang out a succession of merry chimes." The itinerary did not take the Princess past the Oldmachar Poorhouse (Prince Charles Barracks) but the inmates got a splendid view of the procession from a grandstand specially erected for their benefit by Mr J Murray Garden, the owner of Maryfield. Among the umbrellas raised in salute in the distinguished guests' grandstand at the park was that of the Revd James Iverach. The name of the Revd Henry Wright does not appear on the invitation list. Sad.

ACADEMIC INTERLUDE

NOR does he appear to have been involved in the next great event, unlike the Minister of Ferryhill Free Church and James Iverach who by now was Principal of the Free Church College. We have moved to 1906 when the University of Aberdeen chose to celebrate its Quatercentenary. It could be argued that since the University only came into being when King's and Marischal were united in 1860, the celebration was premature. However, the anniversary they had in mind was of the founding of King's College which took place in 1495. So they were really 11 years late, although there had been a comparatively low key event in 1895 linked to the opening of the Mitchell Hall. It was felt that the Quatercentenary merited something more elaborate and it was decided to make another linkage - this time with the completion of the new buildings at Marischal. Up to that time the Marischal quadrangle was hidden behind a row of run down shops and tenements, with access via a small archway. As the spectacular new "wedding cake" facade took shape it must have made a staggering impact. This was a world-beater - the city had seen nothing like it and probably never will again. So to make its official opening the centre-piece of the Quatercentenary celebrations made good sense even if they had to be delayed for a year or two. If the city went gyte for the opening of the Duthie Park, in 1906 the University went mental. The celebrations lasted from 25th to 28th September 1906. Afterwards a book was published recording the details. It weighs more than four and a half pounds. The programme included receptions, dinners, musical and dramatic events, sports, fireworks, "smokers", a students' ball and a service in King's College Chapel. Every university in the world (or so it seems) was invited to send a delegate, and most of them did. Every graduate of Aberdeen University (King's or Marischal) was invited. Interestingly, those who had graduated before 1850 received their invitations in Latin, as did the other universities, honorary graduates and all VIPs with or without title. More recent graduates along with current students and staff received theirs in English. Pause and consider what I have just told you. The University was writing in Latin to people in the farthest corners of the globe in the expectation that they would clear their desks for as long as it took to get to a port of embarkation, sail across the appropriate ocean, find their way to what must have seemed to them an extremity of North Britain, have four days of academic junketing and then go home. Not surprisingly, a few declined. A reply came from New Hampshire from the writer Mark Twain, using his real name: "Mr Samuel Clemens desires to convey his grateful sense of the high honour done him in inviting him to be present upon the occasion of the Celebration of the 400th Anniversary of the founding of the University of Aberdeen, and at the same time to express his profound regret that his circumstances are such as to deny him the pleasure of accepting." In other words, "You must be joking!" Many did accept, possibly influenced by the fact that honorary degrees were to be distributed like after-dinner mints. They included the Prince of Monaco who received a special invitation when it was discovered that at the time of the celebrations he would be sailing down the coast on his way home from an Arctic expedition. In the end of the day very nearly 2000 people said they would come, to which had to be added local dignitaries and university staff. It was going to be a big party. Yes, and the King and Queen were coming.

On the Thursday morning their Majesties arrived at Holburn Street Station - you can still see the platforms. Remarkably their coach drive from the station to Marischal College was recorded on film. As in 1883, the city dressed itself up for the occasion. The weather was fine, which was a blessing because the royal engagement was the inauguration of the new buildings and it took place in the quadrangle. Edward VII doesn't always get a good press. On this occasion he was a star. "His Majesty's first words rang trumpet-like over the vast quadrangle, and with a thrill of delighted surprise the assemblage realised that they had come out not only to see but to hear. The King's fine elocution, more perhaps, than anything else, assured the day's success." The ceremony completed, their Majesties went off to the Town House to have lunch with Lord and Lady Provost Lyon. Had he stayed for dinner, the King could have compared the culinary offerings of two Lyon families - the purveyor for the Strathcona Banquet was J Lyons of Corner House fame. The meal was cooked in London and transported to Aberdeen, accompanied by waiters, on a special train.

By May 1906 over 1300 acceptances to the celebrations had been received. So when in June the octogenarian University Chancellor, Lord Strathcona and Mount Royal, offered to provide a banquet for everyone, there could have been no doubt that caterers would have to be brought in. The University helpfully sent out reminders to non-respondents, and within a few weeks it became clear that Lord Strathcona, who insisted that no expense should be spared, would require to feed 2,500 people. In one place. At one time. In style. It must be assumed that some officer of the university felt obliged to point out that the city contained no venue of anything like the required size. Lord Strathcona's portrait shows a man who had better things to do than be bothered with niggling details. If there wasn't a hall big enough, one would have to be built. The fact that this was June and the banquet was to be held in September simply meant that the hall would have to be built quickly. It was to be a temporary structure. Actually it was for two functions only - the dinner for 2,500 and a reception for 4,500. Marshall Mackenzie, the architect of the new Marischal College, produced designs and within six weeks the Strathcona Hall was built on the site now

Daniel McAndrew Jnr, Sunday School Superintendent at the Free Church. Killed by gas explosion at 22 Polmuir Road.

occupied by Greyfriars House and its car park. The contractors were D Macandrew and Co. Ferryhill has not been mentioned for quite a while in this narrative but we have now touched on a connection. The firm of D Macandrew and Company was founded in 1850 and remained in business until just a few years ago. Around the turn of the century they won many important contracts and did much of the joinery work for the new churches that were being built. Daniel Macandrew Jnr succeeded his father as head of the firm, in partnership with Mr J Alexander Smith. He built Nos 22 and 24 Polmuir Road, moving from 24 to 22 when his family increased. He became Sunday School Superintendent at Ferryhill Free Church. Tragedy struck in June 1893 when, at the age of 37, he was killed by a gas explosion at 22 Polmuir Road. Daniel was thus spared the anxiety of getting the Strathcona Hall built on time in 1906. The building was huge. It was deemed that the top table was further from the main door than guests could be expected to walk, so a carriage drive was constructed. When it came to finding a caterer, it became clear that Messrs Lyons & Co Ltd was the only firm in the kingdom that could cope. The menu was in French, there were six courses, each accompanied by carefully selected wines. Music was provided by a military band and the pipers of the Gordon Highlanders. Grace after dinner was said by the Archbishop of Canterbury. Then came the speeches and toasts. The toasts were certainly drunk (to say nothing of the guests after Sherry, Hock, Champagne, Claret, Port and Liqueurs), but the speeches proved to be inaudible in most parts of the hall. This may have engendered a certain restlessness at some of the tables, particularly those where students and recent graduates were seated. Rounding off the proceedings, Lord Strathcona, obviously aware that there had been an acoustical problem, said: "... I have no doubt that in course of time the good citizens here will be able to find a means of being heard anywhere and everywhere." Incidentally, one of the honorary degrees went to Signor Marconi but he missed the dinner. The immediate aftermath of the Strathcona banquet went straight into student folklore. It is probably quite untrue that a cabbie, delivering a professor who had dined well to his front door and being told by the lady of the house that "This is not my husband" replied "Weel, ye'll hae to mak do wi' him the nicht - he's the only one I've got left." Ferryhill was not untouched by these shennanigans. At the Free Church Manse the Revd Bruce Taylor had Professor Jacob Schipper from

Vienna as his guest. Professor Frank Clarke from the Smithsonian Institution in Washington stayed with Mrs Archibald Forbes in Fonthill Road. Principal Iverach, still staying in Ferryhill Place, had a guest from Budapest, Professor Yanos Kriss. At 9 Fonthill Terrace Mr William Thomson was host to Professor Albert Schatz of Aix-Marseille. Professor Jinzo Matsumura from Tokyo Imperial University stayed with Mr James Troup in Fonthill Road. Ida Thomson, a student delegate from St Andrew's University, stayed at 2 Polmuir Road with Bessie McHardy (daughter of the coal merchant partner of Ellis), an Aberdeen student who later did three years' relief work with the Red Cross in Poland before becoming the principal of a private school in England. Elsewhere, Andrew Carnegie was put up at Ardoe House by the soap manufacturer Alexander Ogston, Sir Edward Elgar was with Professor Sandford Terry at Cults, while His Serene Highness Prince Albert of Monaco settled for bed and breakfast with Major Duncan Gordon at 19 Queen's Road. He would be safe there; Major Gordon was the Chief Constable of Aberdeenshire.

Union Terrace decorated for King Edward VII's visit to the Quatercentenary Celebrations of Aberdeen University 1906.

GILDING THE LILY

JAMES Iverach, like Henry Wright provided his own housing when he arrived from West Calder in 1874. It was not until 1897 that the Free Church congregation acquired a manse - the house next door to the church in Fonthill Road which had been owned by Professor Binnie of the Free Church College. The price paid was £1,450. Several improvements were made to the church building in the early years. A clock and bell were fitted in the tower at a cost of £288 in 1875. In 1879 serious discussion took place regarding possible damage to the spire by passing traction engines. That panic over, in 1883 William Henderson donated a porch which was simply stuck over the existing door. Part of the original arched doorway could be seen until the major alterations undertaken in the winter of 1999/2000. From inside the porch it is still possible to see the shape of the original doorway. The Rose Window was installed in the same year - the gift of James Morrison of Rotunda Cottage (27 Polmuir Road) who had been the kirk's first Treasurer. A donor whose anonymity has been preserved, gave the "Four Gospel" windows in the apse. £1,000 was spent enlarging the hall in 1894, and two years later side galleries were added to the church. This was a controversial matter, vigorously opposed by the architect Duncan McMillan. The original gallery consisted of just a few pews at the top of the staircase - the extension swept right down the church on each side to the south wall, cutting out light from all the windows. McMillan's objection to this darkening of the interior can be understood, but the congregation was growing and it was anticipated that a lot of additional seating would be required. Electric lighting was introduced in 1902 and in the following year a pipe organ costing £900 was installed. It was built to the same specification as that supplied to the millionaire Andrew Carnegie for his Scottish home in Skibo Castle. The arrival of the organ created the church's first redundancy - Mr A W Miller's services as Precentor were no longer required. He was the fourth man to hold this post. The precentor's role was to sing out the first line of each psalm or hymn, preferably in the correct key, and then conduct the singing. In 1892 when Mr Miller was appointed there were 10 candidates for the post. They were put through a kind of public audition and given marks in the presence of the congregation and choir. The first organist was Mr C M Stephen. In 1911

Sir William Henderson

The first three ministers of Ferryhill Free Church: James Iverach (1874-1877), R Bruce Taylor (1900-1906), Thomas B Kilpatrick (1888-1899).

he was succeeded by Irvine Cooper who was to remain at the console for 47 years.

NEXT IN LINE

CONTINUING to review the period during which James Iverach and Henry Wright adorned the Ferryhill scene, the time has come for us to consider the occupants of the Free Church pulpit after 1887 when James Iverach, whose writings had extended his fame beyond the bounds of Scotland, was appointed a professor in the Free Church College. He continued to reside in Ferryhill Place so when the Revd Thomas B Kilpatrick came on the scene, he too had to find somewhere to live - he settled on 7 Marine Terrace. It is likely that William Henderson, with his high-level contacts in Free Church circles, was able to do a little head-hunting, because Thomas Kilpatrick, like Iverach, was a brilliant academic. He was awarded a doctorate by Glasgow University and in 1899 accepted a professorial chair in Manitoba. He is reported to have exercised a deep influence on the Canadian church until his death in 1930. 1899 was also the year in which the Free Church joined with the United Presbyterians to form the United Free Church of Scotland. Minister number 3 was described as "a forceful, genial and breezy personality". Despite that the Revd Bruce Taylor, the first occupant of the kirk's new manse, appears to have been popular during the 7 years of his pastorate. He too was a distinguished scholar and had studied in Germany and Syria. From Ferryhill he moved to a Presbyterian Church in St John's Wood, London. Later he too crossed the Atlantic and eventually became Principal of Queen's University, Kingston, Ontario. Bruce Taylor's Sunday evening class attracted large numbers of young people and his successor, the Revd John Coutts is also described as having "a special genius in addressing young people". He became editor of Youth publications for the United Free Church. His ministry at Ferryhill lasted from 1907 to 1913. Mrs Coutts, who must have been quite a young lady of the manse, lived to be a hundred and in the last year of her life renewed contact with old friends at Ferryhill. The 5th minister, the Revd Millar Patrick, stayed for only three years which mostly fell during the Great War. He came as something of a celebrity having been the editor of the Scottish Students' Song Book. Later he was to play a leading part in compiling the Revised Church Hymnary and the Book of Common Order. Towards the end of his time in Aberdeen the two Ferryhill churches demonstrated that the old divisions were fading by starting to hold joint services during holidays and at other times. Apart from a brief hiccup in 1922 when the UF Session appeared to feel that two month's united worship was excessive, this neighbourliness developed further during the ministry of the Revd David Mair (1918 to 1926) whose "great charm of manner and readiness of utterance" endeared him to both congregations. During his ministry the roll of the UF congregation rose to 900. In 1919 the war memorial windows on either side of the apse were supplied and fitted by the London firm of AL Moore and Son at the expense Baillie William Allan. As has already been noted it fell to David Mair to pen the Press and Journal's obituary for his revered colleague Henry Wright in 1923.

MISSION BEGINS

DR Wright was still in his prime when Alexander Gammie wrote: "Ferryhill Church has had no phenomenal experience in the 32 years of its congregational life. ... If it has made no particular stir and has been comparatively little heard of in the community, perhaps this is, in some measure at least, to be accounted for by the fact that everything has gone smoothly." This comes from Gammie's *The Churches of Aberdeen* and the source of the information was undoubtedly Wright himself - he of the modest and retiring disposition said so little of his own work as to make his church and congregation sound incredibly boring. Gammie believed him and wrote what he wrote. But we know better. The church at the foot of the hill was a busy place throughout the Wright era, with the usual range of organisations all thriving in an environment that put a special emphasis on cultural and literary education. The activities at the top of the hill tended to have a higher profile. It is probably true that the Free Church had become more outward-looking and evangelical in its nature, and the Ferryhill congregation included people who had the means to express this in practical ways. They started a mission school as early as 1879. This was in a room rented from Ross's School in Holburn Street (the site later occupied by the Commercial College). This transferred to Ferryhill

Public School, and stayed there until 1886 when William Henderson provided the funds to build a spacious hall in Wellington Road. This was on a site just south of Bank Street in what we now call South College Street. When this hall was destroyed by fire in 1896 the Sunday School moved back to Ferryhill School. It remained there until 1920 when it merged with the Sunday School that met in the church hall. During the 24 years that the "mission" Sunday School was based at Ferryhill School, and even for a time after it joined the congregational school it continued to be called "The Wellington Road Sunday School" and was referred to in this way in Kirk Session minutes, providing some temporary puzzlement for a future historian. For many years there were 3 Sunday Schools operating - the third being in Bloomfield Road where the church had opened another mission hall at least as early as 1882. It was in the Wellington Road Hall that the kirk's first Mothers' Meeting began, and it was also there that the Aberdeen 1st Company of the Boys' Brigade was launched in 1887. After the Wellington Road fire, the congregation bought a Hall that had been built for mission purposes by Holburn Free Church which had recently moved from Justice Mill Lane (the building is now "Charlie's") to Great Western

The hall at Ferryhill Free Church (now the main hall of Ferryhill Parish Church) set out for the Sunday School.

Road. In 1897 the Bloomfield activities were transferred there and a new Mothers' Meeting got under way. The Bible Woman who had been employed at Bloomfield now moved to the Holburn Street mission. Her salary was paid by Sir William Henderson until his death in 1904. The work at Holburn Street continued until 1928, providing accommodation for a Sunday School, Boys' Brigade and the Mother's Meeting. It is not easy to pin-point the site of the Bloomfield hall which was rented by the church, but the Holburn hall is still to be seen - now known as the Holburn Gospel Hall.

It is clear that from the very early years until 1928, the Free Church, through its missionary activities, was always operating on at least one other site in addition to the main building. References in Kirk Session minutes make it clear that the mission halls were, in effect, satellite churches. In addition to the outreach activities already mentioned, regular Sunday services were held in each of the halls - conducted by volunteers, trainee ministers and the Bible Woman, who probably fulfilled the function of a Deaconess. Clearly there were people who regarded the mission halls as their spiritual homes. It is not easy, after more than a hundred years, to understand why it was necessary to run these halls, at no great distance from the church which was big enough to accommodate all who might want to come. Perhaps people were more conscious of class distinctions, and may have seen them reflected in the houses around Ferryhill. Many of the large mansions still stood in their own grounds. Their owners would have servants and carriages. In the fine new tenements in Fonthill Road and elsewhere, the tenants were mainly tradesmen, shopkeepers and clerks - the middle classes. However, there were also older, more run-down streets and groups of old cottages, all to be demolished in due course. Their inhabitants would have been poor - there was an actual Poor-house in Fonthill Road - and they may have been reluctant, or felt it inappropriate, to join the grander folk in their Sunday best at the kirk. A cynic might say that the better off church members would not be unhappy with an arrangement which kept their less affluent neighbours at arm's length in the mission halls, but this would be an uncharitable interpretation. Certainly at kirk session level there appears to have been a genuine hope that the missions would bring people to the Church - and this wish was fulfilled in many cases. As the area developed, the prominence of the big houses was

John Anderson - for many years a pillar of Ferryhill Free Church. He wrote histories of the Boys' Brigade and the Sunday School.

diminished, better standards of building were achieved all round and the population grew much more homogeneous. The need for a two-tier approach to ministry disappeared, and so did the mission halls.

THE BURRY YEARS

I used the long ministry of Henry Wright at Ferryhill Parish Church to define a period of time on which to focus to find out what was happening in the world, in Aberdeen and the parish of Ferryhill. During most of that time James Iverach continued to play a part in the Free Church - locally as a member of the kirk session and presbytery, nationally as Moderator of the United Free Church General Assembly in 1913-14. Less than six years after Dr Wright died, another long ministry began at the foot of the hill - that of John Burry. He arrived in 1929, retired in 1953 and lived on in Aberdeen until his death at the age of 95 in 1982. So our historical binoculars focus now on the 39 years between the deaths of Doctors Wright and Burry.

By the end of 1923 the Wireless had well and truly arrived. Under the presbyterian authority of John Reith, the British Broadcasting Company had started to revolutionise the way in which people found out what was happening in the world. Newspapers were still important, of course, and there were many more of them than today, but it was from the wireless that they learned of Mussolini's rise to power in Italy, of the death of Lenin and the election of Britain's first Labour government under Ramsay MacDonald, followed two years later by the General Strike. The first decade of John Burry's ministry at Ferryhill saw the Wall Street Crash, the opening of the Sydney Harbour Bridge, the Nazis taking control of Germany under Hitler, the Abdication Crisis and the outbreak of the Second World War. After that nothing would be the same again. There was the Bomb, the Cold War, the Attlee Government, the National Health Service, Television, British Rail, Apartheid, the Coronation - all during the Burry ministry at Ferryhill. During his long retirement Dr Burry witnessed the typhoid epidemic in Aberdeen, saw pictures of the first men on the moon, and heard the news of Kennedy's assassination, Watergate, the troubles in Northern Ireland, the Vietnam War, the emergence of Thatcherism, the death of John Lennon and the Falklands campaign.

Doctors Wright and Iverach left behind a Ferryhill that still had green spaces, but not for long. The extensive gardens of Devanha House had already disappeared. Next came Ferryhill House, in the grounds of which the well known architect and town councillor Scott Sutherland built houses in Bon Accord Street and Ferryhill Road. Deemount Gardens and Avenue were completed. The new Sycamore Place filled up another portion of the old Roy's Nurseries, leaving only a section that would remain as allotments until the 1970's. Above "the plots" the new Great Southern Road was laid out, and with it came the bungalows in Fonthill Gardens. The tramway system from Crown Street to Fonthill Road which had opened in 1903, with a branch to the Duthie Park from 1913, finally closed in 1931. Nearly 70 years later, traces still remain on buildings at the foot of Crown Street and the west end of Fonthill Road - iron brackets to which were fixed cables that gave lateral support to the tram wires.

THE ROBERTSON INTERLUDE

I have referred to John Burry, but someone else came between him and Henry Wright in the ministerial succession at the Parish Church. The vacancy created by Dr Wright's death lasted five months. On 15th May 1924 the Revd Charles Robertson, whose previous charge had been in Little Dunkeld, was inducted. His was to be a short ministry but Charles Robertson and his wife appear to have been a popular couple and a lot was achieved in the space of five years. One of the first duties of the new minister was to preside over the planning of a suitable memorial to his predecessor. January 25th 1925 saw the setting in place of three stained glass windows given by Dr Wright as a tribute to his late wife, plus a further two donated by his sister-in-law dedicated to his own memory. The congregation contributed to the cost of a memorial plaque to the old minister and this was placed in the church vestibule. All the windows and the plaque are now to be seen in the present Ferryhill Parish Church. These five windows are very different in style and execution from the Nativity Window that had been installed earlier and can now be seen in the apse of the present church. The memorial windows were the work of Alexander McLundie who at that time ran the Abbey Studio in Glasgow. They are much admired, and specialists in the field have been inclined to attribute them to a very distinguished artist in stained glass, Margaret Chilton. Enquiries have uncovered the fact that although Miss Chilton spent most of her career in Edinburgh, she was employed from 1918 to 1921 by Alexander McLundie in Glasgow. The Ferryhill windows came a few years later, but may well incorporate some of the designs she produced while working at the Abbey Studio. Dr Wright bequeathed the house at 26 Polmuir Road to the congregation, so it continued to serve as the manse. Other significant events included the creation of a branch of the Woman's Guild in 1926. Music had played a significant part in the congregation's life from its earliest days - we have seen that the pipe organ was part of the original fittings. The church was served well by a succession of capable organists, but choir singing seems to have really taken off with the appointment of George Innes as organist and choirmaster in 1925. Within a matter of months the minister was writing: "The rendering of the musical part of the service from Sunday to Sunday is an increasing delight and inspiration." In 1926 George Innes, who lived conveniently in Affleck House, Affleck Street (he moved to Broomhill Road in 1933), entered the choir for Aberdeen Musical Festival. The adjudicators, Percy Scholes and Plunkett Greene, were great celebrities. They placed Ferryhill first in the class for church choirs - the first of many similar successes. Six months later on 21st November 1926 the choir was broadcasting on the wireless. The transmission from the Cowdray Hall took the form of a sacred concert. Appreciative comments were received from listeners far and near. It is interesting that this involvement in modern technology came ten months before the church was provided with electric lighting. The halls had already been "converted" from gas, but the big switch-on in the sanctuary was part of the Jubilee celebrations in August 1927. The choir continued to thrive under the direction of George Innes. In April 1928 they gave a complete performance of the Messiah, and later that year they were back at the Music Festival. The great Plunkett Greene was again adjudicating, and once more he awarded the Gold medal to Ferryhill. He admired their prepared pieces, but was quite knocked out by their sight-singing: "There were no passengers - not a soul on board that was afraid to shoulder responsibility. They are full of courage and go straight for their work. There was not a single mistake. A remarkable performance and we give them 100 marks." Sight

Ferryhill looking North, around 1962. The Deeside Railway line is still in operation. Part of the famous Round O can be seen top centre just next to the new south hall at Ferryhill South Church. The property developers have not yet absorbed the tennis courts in Polmuir Road and Devanah Gardens. Deemount Gardens has not yet been extended and there are still blank sites in Sycamore Place

The end of an era in public transport. Ferryhill's tram service was replaced by buses - this picture was taken at the foot of Crown Street during the few months when both services operated side by side.

singing disappeared from the festival syllabus many years ago. In 1928, the test piece would, of course, be in sol-fa notation, and all the choristers would have learned, at primary school, to read sol-fa with the help of a "modulator" and a blackboard pointer. After their triumph at the festival it is not surprising to find the Ferryhill Choir being selected to give demonstrations of the new hymns that would appear in the Revised Church Hymnary in 1929. During the thirties the choir took part in festivals throughout Scotland. Perhaps their most notable achievement was in winning the Mearns-Brownlie Trophy at the Glasgow Festival in 1936. George Innes also conducted the famous Hall Russell Male Voice Choir and he was able to persuade some of its stalwart members to join the church choir. A photograph taken after the visit to Glasgow in 1936 shows 17 men and 24 women - quite a choir.

Ferryhill North Church Choir 1936 after winning the Mearns-Brownlie Trophy in Glasgow. Choirmaster George Innes is on Revd Dr Burry's left in the front row.

UNITED YET DIVIDED

1929 was the year in which the union of the United Free Church and the Church of Scotland took place. It was also the year in which the Revd Charles Robertson accepted a call to St Oswald's Church, Edinburgh. Curiously there is no record of his having informed the Ferryhill Kirk Session about this. They knew all about it, and got on with the arrangements, but the Clerk didn't write it down. It seems that the Robertsons remained in Edinburgh throughout the Second World War. Writing many years later the Revd Peter Davidson recalled Charles Robertson as a kindly Convener of the Students' Committee at New College. He was killed by an avalanche while on holiday in Switzerland.

NEW NAMES

BY the time John Burry arrived in Aberdeen from Alves, his new charge had adopted the name Ferryhill North, and the UF Church had become Ferryhill South. All over Aberdeen, congregations which had started as rival representatives of opposing denominations were now part of the same Presbytery and the same Church. Facing each other across the street, standing side by side, even occupying different parts of the same building, the absurdity of the situation didn't seem to occur to anyone. At the time people thought it odd that Woolworths should have two shops within a quarter of a mile of each other. Had the North of Scotland Bank opened branches on opposite corners of Union Street and Market Street, the sanity of the boardroom would have been questioned. (When bank mergers actually did create this kind of possibility branch closures became automatic.) Today the thought that denominational union should lead to congregational union seems no more than common sense. It happened in some places. But in Aberdeen, where the logic of at least moving in the direction of joining neighbouring congregations together seems blindingly obvious, the idea was taken up in only a few cases. On the whole it just did not figure on the agenda. The nettle wouldn't be grasped in Ferryhill for half a century.

When David Mair accepted a call from an Edinburgh congregation he was succeeded at the UF Church by yet another minister who was destined for academic stardom. The Revd Donald McKenzie was a Lewis man who, according to his successor "combined the highest philosophic attainments with Celtic eloquence in a mixture of mysticism and humour and prophetic dogmatism all his own". These gifts were made available to the Ferryhill congregation for a very limited period. Mr McKenzie was granted leave to lecture in the United States. This led to the offer of a chair at the Western Theological Seminary in Pittsburg with the result that the Celtic eloquence from the Ferryhill pulpit was silenced after only 18 months, the last of which saw two significant events take place. First came the controversial decision to close the Holburn Street Mission on the grounds that it had now served its purpose and that its work could conveniently continue in the main church building.

DUNCAN McMILLAN

THE second event was the death of Duncan McMillan, marking the end of an era. He had been one of the group of Free Church stalwarts who founded the congregation, he was the architect of the building, served two long spells as Session Clerk and filled various other roles including that of Sunday School Superintendent. He must have been a man of tremendous energy, perhaps even a restless spirit. Moving from Inverness to Aberdeen to train as an architect, he first lived at 13 Bank Street. Then he moved briefly to Rosemount Place. Around 1871 he built and lived in the first house to be erected in Albury Road (now No 64). Subsequently he moved successively to Numbers 54 and 61 in the same street, then in 1890 to 66 Polmuir Road. In 1897 we find him at 16 Bon Accord Square. Within two years he had moved round the corner to 14 Bon Accord Crescent before he finally came to rest in 1901 at 7 Marine Terrace where he stayed for the rest of his life. Duncan moved his architectural practice almost as frequently as his home. At different periods it was based at Numbers 74, 35a and 211 Union Street before settling at 105 Crown Street. Resignations from the Kirk Session were common during McMillan's lifetime. Numerous individuals who felt thwarted by decisions with which they disagreed simply lifted their lines and departed, presum-

Duncan McMillan, architect and session clerk of Ferryhill Free Church.

ably in high dudgeon. This was not Duncan McMillan's way. The building of side galleries, cutting across the graceful windows of the sanctuary, and the installing of an organ pipe box in front of the apse must have been heart-breaking to him. He made his views known, but accepted the decisions and continued to serve the congregation for the rest of his life. Surprisingly his well deserved memorial plaque was not unveiled for another 20 years.

On 21st October 1928, the Revd Robert Stewart from Cambuslang preached as sole nominee and on 19th December he was inducted as the 8th minister of Ferryhill UF Church. In a sense he was also its last minister because within a year the Union took place, the congregations of Ferryhill became North and South respectively and Mr Stewart found himself first minister of the latter within the Church of Scotland. He was to stay for eight years during which he presided over the kirk's sixtieth anniversary celebrations. His most important personal contribution was to undertake the writing of "A Diamond Jubilee Retrospect".

DEAR JOHN

THROUGHOUT the thirties, the householder at 55 Albury Road provided Ferryhill with an interesting link to Royalty. John Brown bore the same name as his uncle who attained fame, if not notoriety, as the servant and confidant of Queen Victoria. It was his custom to wear, on an Albert chain, the repeating watch which his uncle received from Her Majesty after coming to her assistance when she was involved in a carriage accident. A huge portrait of the famous Highlander had pride of place in the Albury Road residence. It was believed to have hung in Windsor Castle until its removal, along with other memorabilia, when policy dictated that the less said about the Monarch's relationship with John Brown, the better.

MORE ABOUT MISSION

ROBERT Stewart prefaced his Diamond Jubilee Retrospect with lines from Revelation Chapter 11: "Rise and measure the temple of God, and the altar, and them that worship therein." Those that worshipped therein had certainly measured up remarkably well to the challenge of Mission. John Moir, who had the distinction of being the founding captain of the 1st Company Boys' Brigade left for the mission fields of South Africa as early as 1890. From 1922 the congregation supported Effie Sutherland as their "own missionary" on the Gold Coast. In fact the support came annually from a Sale of Work organised by the women's Work Party. Effie Sutherland was a popular figure, having gained her early experience as a Sunday School teacher at the Holburn Street Mission. She remained at her post on the Gold Coast until her retirement in 1947. There were several other members of the congregation who answered the call in far off fields, but the one who achieved the greatest fame, almost celebrity, was Agnes Henderson, daughter of Sir William, Ferryhill Free Church's generous benefactor. Brought up with 9 brothers and sisters in Devanha House, she was educated at the Misses Murray's school in Aberdeen and then at another private school in London. Having formed an ambition to become a medical missionary, she entered the London School of Medicine for Women, qualifying as a doctor in 1889. She took her MD degree in Belgium and then spent some time in Vienna before sailing for India in 1890. By this time her mother had died, proud in the knowledge that Agnes was on course to work in the mission field. Sir William Henderson decided to endow a medical missionary post in India as a memorial to his wife. Agnes was appointed to fill it. After 6 months in Bombay she arrived in Nagpur in North India where she established the Medical Mission which was to be the setting for her life's work. It became one of the leading medical centres in the continent, and the hospital continues to serve a vast community 75 years after Agnes Henderson's death. Her personal sacrifice in developing the mission was well recognised in India. At the time of her death in 1925 a Hindu newspaper said: "By her sweet character she endeared herself to high and low, and by her success in curing her patients she won the confidence of all. Though she is gone, the memory of her selfless life for the good of humanity will never be gone. It will never cease to inspire and to encourage others to follow in her footsteps."

THE HUNGRY THIRTIES

THE 1930s were anxious years. The Wall Street Crash was a dramatic feature of a world-wide economic depression that led to unprecedented levels of unemployment. Aberdeen could not escape from this, nor could the two Ferryhill congregations. Special efforts were continually required to raise additional funds so that the books could be balanced. The shortfalls were of the order that would be regarded as trifling today, but 60 years ago they were matters of real concern. The percentage of the population claiming church membership in 1934 was considerably greater than is the case at the end of the century, but the need to bring even more people into the fellowship was given a high priority. In February 1934 we find Dr Burry urging his people to support Aberdeen Churches Campaign: "Its purpose is to secure a deepened spiritual life and a new or greater devotion to the King and Head of our Church, Jesus Christ our Saviour. Who can say there is no need for this?" The Campaign took the form of meetings held in the Music Hall at 3.00pm and 8.00pm every day for a fortnight. In that same month, the Ferryhill North (Men's) Guild had a lecture on "The Cinema and its Uses" and an exposition by the Revd Robert Stewart, from the neighbouring South Church, on the Soviet State which he regarded as a most exciting experiment. He argued that the Right Reaction ought to be one of abhorrence and alarm at the atheistic doctrine, accompanied by sympathy for the oppressed. There was a lot going on in the kirk at the foot of the hill. Dr Mary Esslemont was the guest speaker at the Woman's Guild and George Innes was still keeping the choir at the forefront of the city's musical life. Affectionately known as "Pop", Mr Innes was quite a disciplinarian. He knew that good performances could not be achieved without full attendances at choir practice every Thursday. The report of the choir's 1934 concert mentions Nan Davidson as the accompanist. Her name was to become very well known as one of the BBC's regular accompanists until the 1950s. Three weeks after the choir concert, the Dramatic Section of the Guild presented at four act pastoral comedy called "A Month of Sundays". However, the outstanding Spring event in 1934 was a Dramatic Recital by the Revd Henry Ironmonger who came to Aberdeen "with a great record of influence and success in England." Despite his apparent celebrity, tickets for Mr Ironmonger's performance were priced at only one shilling, surely a bargain for the chance "to hear masterpieces of English literature sympathetically interpreted and to enjoy clean healthy entertainment blended with humour and pathos". The decade continued with a constant buzz of activity, punctuated by moments of foreboding as the Minister alerted his people to the menace of Fascism in Europe, and helped them to come to terms with the death of King George V and the subsequent Abdication crisis. March 1939 saw a visit to Aberdeen of delegates who had attended the International Missionary Conference at Tambaram in India, described as the most widely representative body of Christians ever assembled. The team, which included church leaders from China and India, was headed by Dr George MacLeod, first leader of the Iona Community. Seven months later, foreboding had become reality, Britain was at war and Dr Burry was writing to the congregation: "The Minister would like it to be known that he is ready to help any who may have conscientious objections to coming within the military machine. The Church of Scotland has declared that both pacifist and non-pacifist positions are held by Christians with equal sincerity."

Meanwhile, up at Ferryhill South, Robert Stewart did not enjoy a particularly comfortable ministry. The decision to close the Holburn Street Mission was taken soon after his arrival, although the signs that it would happen were clear long before that. To describe the decision as conten-

Crown Street newsagent's shop in the 1920s. It shows the one remaining sign of the existence of Dee Village.

tious possibly under-states the disappointment it caused in certain quarters. Resignations and "lifting of lines" followed and it seems likely that some of the congregation's more generous financial supporters departed. By March 1936 the congregation was unable to meet its obligations and the minister was offering to forego the £25 supplement to which he was entitled. This offer was refused, and several years of financial campaigning began. The light at the end of the tunnel was eventually reached in 1938 when the books showed a credit balance of £16 8s 1d. By that time there was a new family at the manse. Robert Stewart left for Dunbartonshire in 1936 and in November of that year the Revd Merricks Arnott arrived from Dumfries to begin a colourful and, at times, controversial ministry. Dr Burry was among those who took part in a welcoming reception, an indication that the two Ferryhill congregations were now living happily alongside each other.

The Revd Robert Stewart takes the salute (around 1935).

FIRST AND TWELFTH

MERRICKS Arnott must still have been attempting to put names to faces in his congregation when he found himself involved in the Jubilee celebrations of the 1st Company of the Boy's Brigade, which was followed a few weeks later by an even bigger jamboree for the Jubilee of the Aberdeen Battalion - this took place in the Music Hall and Ferryhill Old Boys were given prominent roles. Sixty of the 1st Company Old Boys met in the Cowdray Club to swap recollections of the early days. Two of them, Harry Ross and Harry Thomson could go back to the very beginning when the company met in the old Wellington Road Mission Hall under the benevolent eye of Captain John Moir, who later became a missionary in South Africa. The BB started in Glasgow thanks to the inspiration of William Smith who today would be recognised as a marketing genius. He identified a need (to give boys something worthwhile to do) and worked out the perfect way to meet it and to promote it to a wider and wider public. The growth of the organisation was phenomenal. In Aberdeen activities based on the BB system were started at the Porthill Mission in the Gallowgate. John Moir, who was already involved at the Ferryhill Mission School, visited Porthill, liked what he saw and had no difficulty in persuading the Free Church Kirk Session that a fully fledged BB Company should be started. Two weeks later, Rutherford Free Church followed suit, and others followed in fairly rapid succession. The Established Churches were slower to come on board. At Ferryhill Parish Church the 12th Company was founded in 1898. By 1907 the Aberdeen Battalion boasted 40 companies. The 1st Company was 10 years old when the most eventful chapter in its history was written. First, there was an invitation to prepare a gymnastic display at a public meeting in the Trades Council Hall at which the founder of the movement, William Smith, would speak. This was an honour and special practices were immediately arranged - taking place as usual in the Wellington Road Hall. During one of these sessions, something untoward occurred in a side room used to teach cookery to girls. The hall went on fire. The gymnasts were obliged to escape by dashing through a passage that was already a mass of flames. There were no casualties, but the boys lost all their clothing and had to go home in their PT kit. The hall was gone forever. However, preparations for the display continued and in due course William Smith was so impressed that he arranged for the Company to receive an even more prestigious invitation - to represent Scotland at a National Demonstration at the Queen's Hall, London on 7th May 1897. Under the leadership of Lieutenant David Gibson, the vaulting horse team of 12 boys set off on this tremendous adventure. At the Queen's Hall they did Scotland and Ferryhill proud. The 6000 strong audience demanded an encore of their display. On their return to Aberdeen they received an ovation from the crowd awaiting their arrival at the station. This was a special event, and pride in it lasted for many years. The only fly in the ointment concerned the funding. The Company received an advance from the Battalion and, since they were representing Scotland, assumed that other companies would chip in to help them repay the loan. This didn't happen, and the debt "hung like a millstone" round the 1st Company until 1901, and was undoubtedly still a subject for discussion

The team from the 1st Aberdeen BB Company which took part in the 1897 national display in London.

Captain J M Moir, first Captain of the 1st Aberdeen Boys' Brigade Company.

when old boys got together in 1937. The day before they met at the Cowdray Club, Merricks Arnott presided at a concert given by members of the Girls' Association including two comedies and a missionary play. The cast included Mary Marr whose service to the congregation still continues 62 years later. The first few months of the Merricks Arnott ministry also included the silver jubilee of Irvine Cooper as organist. Held in high regard as a conductor (he was for a time the Musical Director of the Lyric Opera Company), Irvine Cooper was also known as a composer and critic. He continued in post at Ferryhill South until the 1950's.

BB recruits are taught Wand Drill by Lietenant Fiddes in Ferryhill School playground in 1907.

MOVIES FOR MISSION

THE distinctive feature of Merricks Arnott's time in Aberdeen was his involvement with young people. Within the Ferryhill congregation we find the formation of a Brownie pack, a Children's Own Meeting and a Junior Bible Class. The Minister is credited with writing a play for the Lifeboys. But two things brought him into more public prominence. The first was his pioneering leadership of the Seaside Mission at a time when the Aberdeen beach was a major mecca for holiday-makers. The Mission ran during the period of the Glasgow Fair and sometimes as many as 3000 people would listen and watch Merricks Arnott and his colleague Mackenzie Grieve from John Knox Gerrard Street. Sometimes they would organise the children to present parable plays on the sands. One of these, "The Pearl of Great Price" was so successful that Merricks Arnott arranged to have it filmed in colour. Colour movies were still a

West Lodge of Duthie Park in 1938. It was later rebuilt in Rubislaw Den South.

Ferryhill from the air in the 1930s. Sycamore Place has yet to be laid out. A blank site in Murray Terrace indicates the proposed location of a railway station - the plan was abandoned.

novelty in 1937. The impression made when the completed film with sub-titles added, was shown in churches, must have been considerable. The use of film in church was the second topic that brought Merricks Arnott into prominence. Of course, the cinematograph had been used in church halls for many years. But he brought it into the Church itself, and this drew criticism. He also made the films himself, proving to be a skilled director and craftsman. The minister's cine camera became a familar sight at Sunday School picnics and other church events. In 1939 he produced a newsreel illustrating all the summer activities of the congregation. He also produced "In the Swim", a two reel colour film featuring the "Ferryhill Fliers", the name by which the kirk's youngsters were known. The outbreak of war prevented it being shown at the Edinburgh Amateur Film Festival. Merricks Arnott provided a copy of "In the Swim" and some other Ferryhill footage for the "Parish Panorama" which formed part of the congregation's Centenary celebrations in 1974.

THE KIRK GOES ON SHOW

IN 1938 Merricks Arnott visited the Empire Exhibition in Glasgow. This vast affair in Bellahouston Park included an "Exhibition Church" which so appealed to the young Ferryhill minister that he resolved to re-invent the idea for his own parish. So it was that in September of that year "Church Week" took place. The concept has been repeated since then, but at the time it was something new and attracted considerable press interest. Every part of the church building was used to house a comprehensive exhibition of everything that regularly happened within its walls. Every church organisation was represented and there was a portrait gallery and tea room. Conducted tours were organised to take people to remote corners to see the organ bellows working and to experience the temperature in the furnace room. Apparently it all went very well. A special illustrated feature appeared in Life & Work in August 1939 in which Merricks Arnott looked back: "After Church Week, the congregation went forward to its winter's work with renewed vigour." Sadly, its effects would be largely dissipated by the black-out, rationing and air-raid warnings - all of which were about to invade the lives of churchgoers and everyone else.

Ferryhill South Church Week Exhibition 1939

Revd Merricks Arnott joins the ladies for tea at the Church Week Exhibition. Mary Marr is on the extreme left.

WAR IS DECLARED

ALTHOUGH not an out and out pacifist like John Burry, Merricks Arnott had to wrestle with his conscience when Britain declared war on Germany. He was quick to offer support and encouragement to men and women who went on active service whether as conscripts or volunteers. Like almost all the ministers in Aberdeen he had already undergone training in Civil Defence with the ARP and in First Aid. Along with the Kirk Session he readily agreed to Ferryhill South being used for daily services during the early part of the war. These were held at 3.00pm and were conducted on a rota system by ministers from churches in the area. Merricks Arnott tried manfully to keep the Church at the centre of people's lives during the dark days that followed. He addressed these words to Christians who felt obliged to adopt the pacifist position of total opposition to the war: "It is up to this minority to be exceedingly active to prevent the rot of war spoiling our spiritual heritage, to foster friendship and the forgiving spirit against the new day when a peace must be made. The minority will be suspect unless it shows greater courage and zeal than those who believe in war."

Even before the declaration of war, the congregation had involved itself in the aftermath of Hitler's annexation of Austria by undertaking to support two refugee children who were accommodated at East Maryfield. The start of hostilities immediately made an impact on the way things were done in all churches. Blacking out the Ferryhill churches was deemed to be impractical, so during the winter months all services and activities that would normally take place in the evening, were shifted to the afternoon. As people became accustomed to the unlit streets and blackout curtains were obtained for the halls, some evening activities, including services, were resumed. Youth organisations had to confine themselves to Saturday afternoons. In 1941 this added to the difficulties of the Guides, because some of the girls had to go to school on Saturday afternoon.

ANY OLD IRON?

AN idea that has been credited (or debited) to Lord Beaverbrook, had a profound effect on the appearance of Ferryhill. Wearing his war-time hat as Minister of Supply he called on the nation to surrender its iron railings to provide materials that could be re-cycled to provide weapons, munitions or aeroplanes. Throughout Britain this met with an immediate and positive response. Vast quantities of iron were accumulated and many graceful, carefully crafted railings were consigned to official scrap-heaps where they remained for the duration of the war and beyond. It seems that the Beaverbrook idea simply didn't work. Either the metal was not the right type, or there were simply not enough foundries to tackle the re-cycling. Anyway, it was a complete waste of time, effort and money. Churches were not exempt from this patriotic vandalism. In 1950 the Ministry of Works offered Ferryhill South Church the princely sum of £16:7:6d as compensation for its fine railings and gates!

Although the city of Aberdeen suffered quite badly from air-raids, its appearance was altered much more significantly by Lord Beaverbrook than by Hitler. All the granite terraces that made up the west end of the city - Rosemount, Rubislaw, Holburn, Mannofield, Ferryhill - were designed to have iron railings. Many feu charters required house-owners to ensure that such railings were maintained. They all disappeared during the war. Perhaps the victorious troops returning home in 1945 liked the more open, less cluttered appearance of the city. There has certainly never been any serious move to replace railings and the Deacons' Court of Ferryhill South spent the £16:7:6d on something else.

Church life continued remarkably normally despite the war. Minor inconveniences, like having to take your own sugar when there was to be a cup of tea, were accepted cheerfully. Enforced changes in the timing of meetings and services did not prevent congregational activities from proceeding almost as usual. In 1940 the Ferryhill South Kirk Session wrote to the Town Council expressing the view that all children should be evacuated from parts of the city thought to be particularly vulnerable to enemy attack. Presumably Ferryhill was not regarded as being at risk, because the Session was continuing to support the proposal to bring refugee children to stay in the parish. Many church members were involved in work on the home front - in the ARP, Home Guard, WVS and so on. Volunteers helped to run canteens for the forces, and lots of knitting went on to provide "comforts" for the troops. The Emergency Services Committee which was formed at Ferryhill South sent Christmas parcels to all men and women in the services who were linked to the congregation. In 1943 this meant making up 150 parcels. Each one contained, amongst other things, a pullover. How acceptable this was to those serving under the blazing African sun is not noted, but the kind thought would have been appreciated. Both Ferryhill churches were identified by the authorities as Rest Centres. This was the name given to a place of safety for people bombed out of their homes. Halls were fitted out with beds and emergency supplies and lists were prepared of volunteers willing to stand by to offer assistance should the Luftwaffe unload bombs in the area. Mercifully these facilities were never required, but Aberdeen did suffer from many air-raids and there was considerable damage in other parts of the city. A stray bomb landing on the tenements in Crown Street could have been disastrous, so establishing the Ferryhill Rest Centres was by no means a pointless exercise. There was a minor hiccup when the ARP insisted that the centre at Ferryhill South be activated at 12 noon during an exercise to be held on a Sunday. The Kirk Session expressed its displeasure at the timing but agreed that the morning service on that day should be abbreviated!

Possibly because many of the men were absent on active service, an important Sunday morning duty at Ferryhill South was undertaken by the Life Boys during the wartime years. Every week, four boys were detailed to stand at the inner entrances to the church, two downstairs and two upstairs, to open the doors for worshippers. The "Door Boys" were also given the tasks of turning over the pew cushions after each service and placing a protective cover over the pulpit.

A NEW ARRIVAL

MIDWAY through the war, Merricks Arnott received a Call to a parish in Glasgow. Since 1874, 9 ministers had come and gone at Ferryhill South, while down at Ferryhill North they were only at number 3 - Dr Burry was still going strong. His new colleague and neighbour, George Rendle Leathem, was destined to stay for 24 years. His previous charge was at Newburgh in Fife but he was no stranger to Aberdeen. His father had been minister of Holburn Central Church before moving to Canada. Rendle Leathem remained a bachelor and he made several extended trips to Canada to visit his family and to enjoy the role of uncle to a growing number of nephews and nieces. He had a slight disability which necessitated the wearing of a heavy surgical boot, but this did not deter him from the regular visiting of the congregation. Pulpit announcements would indicate the elder's district into which he was to foray in a particular week. He was much loved, and the visits were appreciated, but it was generally understood that the announcements also signalled the days on which his housekeeper would not be required to prepare his evening meal! Perhaps because of his disability Rendle Leathem never became a motorist. Instead he made much use of taxis and buses. Bus journeys were a special delight. If he found a kent face among his fellow passengers he would immediately commence a conversation even if the length of the bus separated him from his quarry. Shyer members of the congregation frequently found this embarrassing, even to the point of getting off the bus several stages earlier than planned, but it provided free entertainment and, quite often, enlightenment for the other passengers. He knew his people well and had a remarkable memory for their family details. He also knew if they had been in church on Sunday morning. It was his practice, during the first hymn, to make eye contact with everyone assembled before him, and to count heads. His whole life revolved around the Church, and he took the closest possible interest in all its organisations.

John Burry, too, was a conscientious and attentive pastor although less at ease in ordinary conversation. However, his Canadian wife, Loreen, had a much more easy-going personality and made the Ferryhill North manse a friendly, welcoming place as well as home to a very large family. During the war Dr Burry was obliged, like Rendle Leathem, to do his visiting by bus, tram and on foot. The Revd James Lindsay Wilkie, who was a Sunday School pupil at the time recalls the Ferryhill North minister "... faithfully visiting his flock through the blackout in his black boots. Because of his pacifism he preached a Gospel many folk did not want to hear in those Churchillian days, and congregations grew less. However he

FERRYHILL SOUTH CHURCH.

Induction of Rev. G. RENDLE LEATHEM, B.D.

WELCOME MEETING IN THE CHURCH HALL.

WEDNESDAY, 29th SEPTEMBER, 1943

Rev. JOHN RANKINE M.A., presiding.

TEA WILL BE SERVED FROM 7 TO 7.30 P.M.

Programme.

PRAISE—"O God of Bethel." - PRAYER.

CHAIRMAN'S REMARKS.

Presentation to the Rev. G. RENDLE LEATHEM, B.D.
Robing by Miss ANNIE OGILVIE and Miss EDITH MILNE.

Remarks—DR. ROBERT RICHARDS.

Remarks—D. M. ADAMSON, Esq., Newburgh.

Remarks—Rev. R. P. CONSTABLE, B.D., Balmerino.

Song—Mrs. BUCKLEY.

Remarks—Rev. W. W. GAULD, M.A.

Remarks—Rev. H. CUMMING, M.A., Forfar.

Remarks—Rev. G. RENTON BROWN, Greenock.

Song—Mrs. BUCKLEY.

Remarks—Rev. C. M. ROBERTSON, M.A., Edinburgh.

Remarks—Rev. J. H. BURRY, B.A., M.D., C.M.

Presentations to—Rev. JOHN RANKINE, M.A., by J. A. MINTY, Esq.
H. THOMSON, Esq., by HUGH R. BARR, Esq.

Votes of Thanks—J. Ross McMILLAN, Esq.

DOXOLOGY. - BENEDICTION.

Note—Please bring your own sugar.

Note the war-time request to "bring your own sugar".

persevered in his loving service of his people, tramping up and down tenement stairs, and by sheer dogged determination and many, many hours of labour, brought the congregation through the war in good heart and ready for peace".

Revd Rendle Leathem gets measured for an apron. Why?

POST-WAR PURSUITS

THE end of the Second World War did not bring an immediate return to the Good Old Days. Austerity and rationing continued for several years. The letters BOC&S still appeared on tickets for the Sunday School picnics to signify that you were expected to bring your own cup and sugar. Both Ferryhill congregations made efforts to welcome and re-integrate men and women returning from the services, and both had names to add to their war memorials. Attempts were made at Ferryhill South to establish a fellowship for ex-service personnel. It didn't work. Probably most of the potential members were only too glad to put their service years behind them and get on with their post-war lives. It is likely too that Rendle Leathem and his civilian kirk session misunderstood the nature of the comradeship that developed in the forces. They probably recalled 1914-18 when almost everyone served in France. The Second World War was fought on many fronts. Lasting friendships were formed between people who had served together in the same theatre of war. Back home again, the mere fact that they had been "in the forces" was not sufficient to bind people with vastly different wartime experiences into a new church organisation.

Considered in the context of an average person's lifetime, the five years taken up by the Second World War was a comparatively short period. But it was much more than an interruption of the nation's normal business. It proved to be a catalyst for change in all aspects of life. Nothing would ever be the same again. Just as the railings disappeared for good, so did the dole queues of the thirties, so did deaths from tuberculosis, so did the idea that middle class households should employ servants, and so, although more slowly, did the linked notions that men were entitled to the best jobs and the best pay and that domestic chores were the sole responsibility of women. The War interrupted normal business, but its interruption of family life produced an even more marked effect on society. The "baby boom" of the immediate post-war years produced a population bulge that resulted in successive needs for post-natal facilities, schools, further education, youth employment policies, housing - and in a few years from now the babies of the bulge will bring about a steep rise in the sum required for the payment of retirement pensions. These changes affected the whole nation - Aberdeen as much as anywhere. The returning service personnel required housing for themselves and their new families. The responsibility to meet this need largely fell to the Town Council. Estates of pre-fabricated houses sprang up to provide temporaray accommodation in various parts of the city. Designed to last only a few years, the pre-fabs which came complete with very modern refinements like refrigerators, remained part of the Aberdeen landscape for much longer than intended. Meanwhile the Council undertook huge building programmes, transforming large areas on the outskirts of the city where, in pre-war years, there had been nothing but farmland. Soon the names Northfield, Mastrick, Garthdee and Kincorth were being displayed on the sign-boards of corporation buses. Families who had been condemned to overcrowded, insanitary conditions in run-down tenements like Black's Buildings and in the ill-famed Castlehill Barracks were re-housed, and not before time. Ferryhill did not change much during this period. Most of the area had already been developed prior to 1939. There were some gap sites available for private housing - Deemount was an example. On the whole, however, further development of Ferryhill did not take place until the 1970s, when the part of Roy's Nurseries which had remained as allotments was purchased by Bredero to build extensions to Brunswick Place and Sycamore Place.

The idea that Aberdeen only became a busy place after the discovery of North Sea oil is misconceived. The city to which the ex-service personnel returned after the war was a bustling community. There was virtually full employment. The building tradesmen were working flat out to complete the new housing schemes. Traditional industries like fishing, textiles and granite were booming. Every summer the beach acted as a magnet for thousands of holiday-makers from the West of Scotland, making Aberdeen

Lord Provost Graham congratulates the Dons on winning the League Championship in 1955. Visible L to R: Archie Glen, Graham Leggat, Harry Yorston, Paddy Buckley, Jack Hather

the most popular resort in Scotland. Military bands played daily throughout the summer on the bandstands at the beach and at Hazlehead. Weekend performances were given at the Duthie Park. Hazlehead was also the location of a marionette theatre which attracted enthusiastic audiences of children. The popularity of the cinema reached its zenith. Queues stretched along Rosemount Viaduct whenever Harry Gordon was due to appear at His Majesty's Theatre. House Full signs were frequently displayed at the Tivoli for summer shows featuring comedians like Jack Milroy and Jimmy Wallace, while at the Beach Pavilion variety bills included such old-timers as Peter Dawson and Dave Willis along with the up and coming talents of Julie Andrews and Benny Hill. Crowds flocked to the greyhound racing stadium at Bridge of Dee, thousands of Aberdonians packed the Mannofield cricket ground to see the great Don Bradman, and at Pittodrie it was not uncommon for reserve team games to attract attendances of over 10,000, a figure that could be multiplied by 3 or 4 for first team matches. The Dons won the Scottish Cup in 1947 and continued to challenge for honours throughout the 50s with players whose names can still be conjured with - George Hamilton, Harry Yorston, Don Emery, Paddy Buckley, Archie Glen, Tommy Pearson, Jack Hather - to name but a few. Ballroom Dancing was a popular recreation. Discos were unheard of. Live bands played nightly at the Palais in Diamond Street, the Locarno in George Street, the Plaza in Spring Garden and the Boulevard in Park Street. Saturday nights provided many more opportunities for tripping over your partner's feet - Madame Murray's at the Cowdray Hall, Donalds' Ballroom in Silver Street, BB Headquarters, Student Hops at the Union and the Mitchell Hall, St Katherine's Club and various other halls. The reopening of the Beach Ballroom made it the city's premier venue for dancers. Blanche Coleman's All Girls Band preceded a long period of residency by Leslie Thorpe and his Orchestra. On Sunday evenings the Ballroom became a variety theatre - the programme always included a Quiz hosted by the popular Beach Leader, Bill Ramsay. Almost half a century later a few of the activities mentioned in this paragraph still survive, probably on a reduced scale. Most have disappeared altogether. People now enjoy themselves in different ways and in different places, thanks to television, the motor car and cheap air travel. It would be unfair to regard these three as culprits. They have brought great benefits. However, they have undoubtedly also led to the total demise of some activities and the diminution of others. One of the institutions that has suffered is the Church.

THE KIRK FIGHTS BACK

IT must be said that the Kirk was beginning to take knocks before the new technology took its toll. The dimensions of 19th Century church buildings probably give us an exaggerated view of church attendance. The aftermath of the Disruption in Aberdeen produced a plethora of vast buildings, each one of which might be well filled on Communion Sundays, and half-empty on most other occasions. As the 20th century progressed, the social obligation to attend worship regularly diminished. The Second World War brought an acceleration of this trend, and also found the Church losing its grip on Sabbath observance. Sunday concerts and film shows became commonplace as did a whole range of sporting and recreational activities that had hitherto been taboo on the Sabbath. Added to these social changes was the fact that the new housing schemes drew people far away from their city centre churches. Of course the Church Extension Scheme did something to tackle that particular problem, but in the 1950s the city centre of Aberdeen was still knee deep in churches, while the mass of the people had moved to the peripheral areas with, if they were lucky, a prefabricated hall church to serve a huge parish. Against this background, the two Ferryhill churches did remarkably well. Numbers did decline, but crept up again. By the mid 50s Ferryhill South and Ferryhill North each had around 1300 members on their rolls. Of these perhaps 800 would be recorded as having received Communion at least once a year, but probably no more than 300 would be regular attenders.

Thanks to its ecclesiastical history, Aberdeen was still seriously over-churched, and this applied in Ferryhill as much as anywhere. Thanks to human nature, the obvious solution would not be achieved for many years, so two large buildings that were rarely full to capacity continued to serve the spiritual needs of the Ferryhill folk. But if the vast sanctuaries had plenty of empty pews available on Sundays, the capacities of the halls were

A busy Joint Station at the start of the Aberdeen Trades Holiday around 1950. The Lemon family from Deemount Gardens are at the barrier.

stretched to the limits on weekdays to cope with the spatial requirements of all kinds of organisations, particularly those catering for the younger generation. Lack of land and money were the obvious obstacles to the necessary expansion. At Ferryhill South, James Ross McMillan (son of the architect of the church) saw the way to a solution. He is recorded as saying: "Since we can't extend to the north, east and west, it is absolutely vital to future generations that we hold the property on our southern boundary." In a gesture of astounding generosity, when 2 Polmuir Road came on the market in 1947, he purchased it and gave it to the church. Part of the back garden attached to this property was earmarked for an additional church hall. It took 15 years for the plan to reach fruition. The new South Hall and ancillary accommodation were completed in 1962 and dedicated on the church's 88th anniversary. The total cost was less than £12,000, but it used up two bequests and the proceeds of the re-sale of 2 Polmuir Road - and still a direct appeal to members had to be made. With the benefit of hindsight, the decision to sell the house can be seen as injudicious. It deprived the congregation of an asset which, in a few years, would have appreciated out of all recognition when the discovery of North Sea oil sent property values in Aberdeen sky high. However, the extra accommodation gave an instant fillip to congregational life and paved the way for a successful Stewardship Campaign in 1963-64, with a follow up in 1965.

At Ferryhill North the long ministry of John Burry came to an end with his retirement in 1953. He continued to live in Aberdeen and remained a respected figure in the community until his death at the age of 95 in 1982. Dr Burry's pacifist beliefs cannot have been shared by his successor the Revd Tom Scott. He had served as a Padre in the RAF during World War 2. Unlike his rather shy predecessor, Tom Scott had an outgoing personality and he was happy to encourage social activities such as dances and concerts. He was a moderniser. It was during his ministry that the tradition of elders appearing at Communion in frock coats and white ties was abandoned. The new broom continued sweeping to the satisfaction of most people for five and a half years, at which point Mr Scott decided to return to a wartime stamping ground by accepting a Call to serve the Church in Kuala Lumpur. Rendle Leathem acted as Interim Moderator for ten months until another longish ministry began with the arrival in March 1960 of the Revd Peter Davidson.

A MAN CALLED PETER

PETER Davidson belonged to that generation of ministers who, having seen active service in World War 2, were permitted by the Church to undertake an accelerated course of training. At that time the normal academic preparation for the ministry was an MA degree followed by postgraduate theological study which often led to the degree of BD. The ex-servicemen were allowed to shorten the arts course and get started to the divinity course a year early. This was an advantage because it enabled

Revd Peter Davidson

them to begin their work as ministers sooner than their contemporaries who took the full arts course. The drawback was that since they had not graduated MA, they were not permitted to graduate BD either, because in those days the BD was regarded as a second degree. Thus it was that the new Ferryhill minister was simply the Revd Peter Davidson and had no letters after his name. This was of no consequence to anyone, of course, but like all ministers who went through this type of training, he felt just a little aggrieved that, having taken the full Divinity course and passed the same exams as everyone else, he was not entitled to the BD degree. He may have lacked an academic label, but Peter Davidson brought ten year's ministerial experience to Ferryhill, not to mention the leadership qualities he had developed as a Sergeant in the Royal Engineers. Persuasive, persistent and perceptive, he was good at spotting untapped talent, and found ways of maintaining a lively congregational life at a time when many churches were in decline. He contrived to do this while contributing much to the work of Aberdeen Presbytery to which he acted as Clerk for several years. Accepting the fact that the Presbytery's plan for adjusting parishes in the city would affect Ferryhill, he prepared his flock for the inevitable union with their neighbours at the top of the hill.

STEWARDSHIP CAMPAIGNS

IN 1963 both Ferryhill congregations responded to a call from the General Assembly to encourage the Christian Stewardship of money, time and talents. Committees were formed and quite elaborate campaigns were planned. The aim was to create a new enthusiasm among the membership in the hope of giving people responsibilities suited to their interests, thereby securing a greater sense of commitment to the Church. There were also hopes that the Kirk's finances would benefit - these were days of increasing inflation and the real value of congregational giving tended to decrease year on year. The basis of the campaigns in both churches was a systematic visitation of every household - this being carried out by teams of visitors who had undertaken special training for the purpose. At the heart of the campaigns there were Stewardship Meals. The Ferryhill North people gathered in the Music Hall, while the Beach Ballroom provided a venue for Ferryhill South. These were not entirely isolated efforts. Follow up campaigns were organised and the Stewardship concept has never died. Nevertheless, the architects of the campaigns were probably disappointed with the results. Undoubtedly many people offered to put their talents at the disposal of the Church. But these offers did not necessarily match the needs at the time, and there were no adequate mechanisms in place for diverting willingness to help into more useful directions. The Stewardship Campaigns did have some success in financial terms. Givings rose appreciably, but the idea of annual (upward) review never really caught on, and the idea that good Stewardship would render obsolete all other fund-raising activities remained a pipe dream. However, there were many positive results. Young Woman's Groups were formed, both congregations started to hold services in residential homes for the elderly, seat rents were abolished and parish magazines were delivered to homes rather than collected at church. The notion that everything in a congregation had to be done by the minister or the elders began to get dispelled.

Ferryhill South Stewardship Meal in the Beach Ballroom 1963

CELEBRATING WHAT?

IN 1967 the Committee of the Ferryhill South Mothers' Meeting decided to make a weekly collection of 3d from each member to defray the costs of a dinner to be held in the Pharos Restaurant in January 1968. This was the month identified by the office-bearers as marking the Jubilee of the Mothers' Meeting. A Jubilee usually signifies a 50th anniversary. In fact the the Mothers' Meeting reached 80 in that year since its origins go back to the early days of the Wellington Road hall. If the re-opening in Holburn Street were taken as the starting date, the 70th anniversary would have fallen in the same year. The transfer of the Meeting to the Church Hall in 1928 might have been celebrated, but that would have been a 40th anniversary! Whatever they were celebrating in 1968, the members did so with much enjoyment and demonstrated their generosity of spirit by presenting the church with a comfortable armchair for use in the vestry.

END OF THE LEATHEM YEARS

LIKE his predecessors in the North Church, Peter Davidson was a happily married man, and his wife Betty was a perfect example of the traditional Lady of the Manse, accepting multifarious responsibilities, generally being taken advantage of, and, for much of the time, taken for granted. Rendle Leathem was frequently the recipient of their hospitality until in 1967 he accepted a call to Springfield in Fife. Re-adjustment was still some distance away, and the Ferryhill South Congregation was permitted to call a minister "without restriction". Their choice fell on Robert Whiteford, a wartime naval chaplain who had served parishes in Rhynie and Neilston. He was a keen sportsman and had achieved distinction on the rugby field in his younger days. After 23 years of bachelor occupancy, the Manse at 54 Polmuir Road became a family home again. The Whitefords had a daughter and three sons, all living at home at the start of their father's ministry in Ferryhill.

CENTENARIES

WITHIN a few years of the Whitefords' arrival, both congregations found themselves in the throes of centenary celebrations. At Ferryhill North, a programme of events lasting a fortnight began in October 1973 with a Centenary Family Service which saw the return of two previous ministers, Thomas Scott and John Burry. Flower containers and seats were installed at the front of the church and table lecterns, made by one of the elders, Sandy Reid, were donated to Westbank, Polmuir Road and Ferryhill Place residential homes. Social events included a "Good Old Days" variety show and a celebration dinner held in the Queen's Hotel. This event was announced almost apologetically by the organising committee : "The cost will be around £1.66. This figure might

Revd Robert Whiteford presents a cheque to the Moderator of the General Assembly (Dr David Steel) after the Ferryhill South Centenary Service 1974.

seem high to some folk." Less than a year later the Ferryhill South congregation marked their hundredth anniversary by creating a new room in the space previously filled by the gallery in the North Hall and raising funds to provide much needed equipment at the maternity hospital in Jalna, India where their missionary partner, Mary Wilson, worked as matron. At a reception following the centenary service, a telephone conversation between the Moderator of the General Assembly of the Church of Scotland, the Rt Revd David Steel (who had been guest preacher), and Miss Wilson in Jalna was relayed to the congregation. The other major event in the celebrations was "Parish Panorama", an ambitious pageant-type entertainment using drama, music, slides and film to recount the history of the congregation. A highlight was the showing of one of the colour films made by Merricks Arnott in the 1930s and featuring "the Ferryhill Flyers".

GENTLEMEN AND LADIES . . .

THE second century of Ferryhill South was not long underway when, heedless of John Knox's warning about the "monstrous regiment", the Kirk Session took the historic step of appointing women elders. There had been a little hesitation. The Session's first response to the General Assembly's enabling legislation had been to say "Yes, but not now". This position could not be sustained for long in view of the obvious quality of the female leadership in the congregation, and on 9th March 1975 sixteen women were ordained to the eldership. The reasoning behind ordaining so many at one time appears to have been that it was right to ordain every woman who was still active in the congregation and who would, by that time, have become an elder had the law of the Church permitted it. Ferryhill North took a more cautious approach, deciding to ordain only three women in the first instance. The feminist cause was not completely won at Ferryhill South. Credence was given to a claim that the counting of the Sunday offering had been thrown into chaos since women became involved. A new system was introduced involving a rota of handpicked tellers. Needless to say, when the talents of volunteers were assessed, women formed the majority in the chosen team.

COMMUNITY OF INTEREST

BY the early 1970s the holding of joint services during the summer months had become firmly established, but thoughts of linking the two Ferryhill congregations in any other way were still not much more than glows on the back burner. Oddly enough it was an Act of the Westminster government which provided an opportunity for the united action, although not in an ecclesiastical area. The Secretary of State for Scotland introduced a scheme for the formation of Community Councils. In Aberdeen it seemed likely that Ferryhill would be in the forefront, because the area already possessed a strong community spirit and had many of the characteristics of a "village" in the centre of the city. However, when the draft scheme was published the boundaries proposed for Ferryhill included not only the Duthie District Ward (which most people thought of as Ferryhill), but the whole of Gairn as well, plus a little of the Central ward which took in part of Union Street. Representations were made to restrict the area to the Duthie ward, but they fell on deaf ears. The final scheme published in 1976 called for a Community Council of 12 members, 6 to be elected from Duthie and 6 from Gairn. The essential first step was for 20 electors to sign a petition calling for elections to be held. Since nothing happened spontaneously, the matter was taken up by the Kirk Sessions of Ferryhill North and South Parish Churches. They agreed to provide signatures for the petition and to see that enough candidates would be forthcoming to ensure that a Community Council could be formed. In the event, 6 people were nominated for Gairn so all were returned unopposed. Duthie produced 8 or 9 candidates and, in due course, an election was held. Although the Council was non-religious and non-political from the start, the interest of the two kirk sessions was reflected by the fact that 8 of the 12 members were active church workers, 5 from Ferryhill South and 3 from Ferryhill North, including the Lady of the Manse, Betty Davidson. The first Chairman and Vice Chairman of the Council were Ferryhill South elders, David Haggart and Jimmy Shearer. An early initiative was the founding of the Senior Citizens' Lunch Club which opened for business on a weekly basis in the North Church Hall. At the start the meals were provided by the proprietor of the Crossroads Fish Restaurant in Crown Street, but it was not long before a team of volunteer helpers became responsible for the catering themselves.

At the time Ferryhill was something of an "artists' colony" with several distinguished painters and sculptors living locally. This inspired the Council to hold an Arts and Crafts Exhibition in Fairfield House. One of Scotland's most distinguished painters, Ian Fleming, lived in Fonthill Road. He took a great interest and for several years was responsible for "hanging" the exhibition with the able assistance of his next door neighbour and fellow artist, Ian Stuart. The exhibition became established as a regular feature of the Ferryhill calendar. After the closure and demolition of Fairfield House it moved to Devanha House for several years before finding a permanent home in Ferryhill Parish Church.

The Community Council's highest profile events in its early years were the Galas held in the Duthie Park. A marquee was hired to house a Children's Art Exhibition, Floral Art and Home Baking Competitions. At the south end of the park an area was fenced off for children's races and the central area was laid out for a five-a-side football tournament. Music was provided by the Stoneywood Works Band (now UDI Aberdeen City Band). Other attractions included a display of vintage motor cars, performances by the Aberdeen Gunfighters, karate displays and a variety of fairground side-shows. The 1983 gala coincided with the Centenary of the Duthie Park. On that occasion people were encouraged to attend in Victorian dress - and prizes were awarded. On another occasion there was a display by a local group who specialised in Polish Dancing in traditional costume. This proved very popular and the dancers were invited to take part in another event - a Community Concert which drew a packed audience to Harlaw Academy. Local choirs and ensembles were much to the fore in the concert, but one of the solo artistes was a very young Murray McLachlan, now internationally known as a concert pianist, but playing classical guitar on that occasion.

It was not all fun, however. At a packed meeting in Ferryhill School the Chairman had to pour oil on some very stormy waters when local residents objected to the Church of Scotland's proposal to use Deeford House as a centre for the treatment of men recovering from addiction to alcohol.

The Council had some successes as a pressure group acting on behalf of the community. One example was the provision of traffic lights at the Springbank Terrace/Bon Accord Street junction. Another achievement came when the Council managed to persuade the authorities that a mistake

Story Time and Music Making at Ferryhill South Sunday School in 1975. The visitor is the Revd Ian Macaulay from the Presbytery Education Committee.

had been made in granting planning permission for a scheme to build houses in the area previously covered by allotments in Sycamore Place/Brunswick Place. While construction was going on it was noticed that the footpath which formerly led through "the plots" to Great Southern Road had disappeared. Reference to old maps showed that it was a well established Right of Way. The developers were obliged to re-design the scheme so that the citizens of Ferryhill could once again enjoy the short cut!

Having seen the Community Council firmly established, most of the members with strong church connections felt able to step back and allow others to continue the work. In some parts of the city Community Councils never became established, and in some areas where they were set up, interest declined and councils went defunct, but in Ferryhill, throughout the 80s and 90s there were always enough volunteers to keep things going. Links between the Community Council and the Kirk were maintained in various other ways, including the organising of Songs of Praise events when the Duthie Park galas were revived in 1998 and 1999, and the adoption of the church hall as the venue for the Community Arts exhibition.

Members of the Woman's Guild in Ferryhill North Church celebrated the Jubilee of their branch in 1976, receiving friendly congratulations from the South branch, seven years their junior. Back in 1926, the Woman's Guild started up in Ferryhill North at a time when something else called The Guild was still one of the congregation's leading organisations. As we have seen, this was a social/educational club founded during Henry Wright's ministry. The Woman's Guild and The Guild appear to have co-existed without confusing anyone other than future historians until the Second World War.

OIL

SINCE the two Ferryhill churches were founded in the 1870s, Aberdeen has never stood still. Each successive generation witnessed changes, but the realisation that the oil deposits under the North Sea could be exploited commercially brought about an acceleration of change. From the mid 1970s Aberdeen became a much more cosmopolitan place as, one by one, international oil companies set up branches in the city. Soon some of the major companies established European headquarters, transferring staff from the United States, the Middle East, Holland, France and Germany. The city's education provision was affected. An American School opened in Cults, and special arrangements were made for French and Dutch pupils to be taught in their own languages. New hotels were built and others extended to cope with the influx of business visitors. Relaxation of the licensing laws brought about a proliferation of bars, lounges and night-clubs. For the first time the taste-buds of Aberdonians were tempted by the delicacies served in the exotic styles of China, India, France, Italy, America, Mexico and Turkey. Even at Esslemont and McIntosh's, for long very much an "establishment" shop, the restaurant switched to a Scandinavian menu. As it became clear that Oil was to be more than a nine day wonder, house-building proceeded apace, leading to the creation of what was virtually a new town at Bridge of Don, with substantial residential developments at various other locations including Cove Bay, Portlethen Cults, Culter, Dyce

The last day of hot metal printing at Aberdeen Journals in 1979. The man with the smart tie is David Walker, a well known Ferryhill personality.

and Westhill. The churches reacted to this. In two places this involved ecumenical cooperation. At Westhill, the new Trinity Church was shared between the Church of Scotland, the Episcopal Church and the Roman Catholic Church. At Bridge of Don, St Columba's Church became home for congregations of the Church of Scotland and the Roman Catholic Church. Elsewhere, American oil exiles played a big part in the creation of the International Baptist Church at Cults, and the Congregational Federation planted churches at Danestone, Balmedie and Cove Bay. Much later new Church of Scotland congregations were established at Cove Bay and at Ashwood Park, where Oldmachar Parish Church became the second church to serve the Bridge of Don area. The initial scarcity of accommodation when the oil families first arrived led almost overnight to an explosion in house prices, bringing them to an unprecedented level which put Aberdeen on a par with Edinburgh and London. This was good news for builders, solicitors and vendors, but not so good for people outside the affluent oil industry, especially if they were first time buyers. Couples who, in the 1960s, would have set up home in a three bedroomed terraced house, found that their budgets in the 70s and 80s would stretch no further than a single bedroomed top floor flat. New building and the government's policy of encouraging people to buy their council houses brought about a rapid increase in home ownership, and with it more subtle changes in the fabric of society in neighbourhoods. Ferryhill didn't look much different on the outside, but many houses that had previously been occupied by families, were split up to provide accommodation for single people and working couples. So the parish profiles of both congregations changed. Members who had resided in the parishes, moved to the newer housing areas. Many of them retained their links with the kirk, but often at a reduced level. Their old homes in Ferryhill were purchased by incomers. Neither congregation succeeded in attracting many of the new people, so the congregational rolls went into slow decline. Each congregation did, however, have a nucleus of committed members and attendances at Sunday worship remained reasonably healthy. Some of the larger houses in the area were converted to form residential homes for the elderly. The two Ferryhill churches willingly accepted the challenge of conducting regular Sunday evening services in these homes. The ministers sometimes took part, but in the main the services were led by elders and other members of the congregations.

COMETH THE HOUR COMETH THE MAN

AFTER 14 years at Ferryhill South, Bob Whiteford accepted a call to the Orkney parish of Shapinsay. Aberdeen Presbytery's Union and Readjustments Committee tried to persuade the office-bearers of the North and South churches that the time had come to think seriously about uniting. The matter was discussed for many months , during which time the Revd Walter Gordon proved to be a most acceptable locum. Many people could see the sense of the proposed union, but agreement was not reached and eventually Ferryhill South was given permission to call a minister. Thus it was that the Revd Ian Dick and family took occupancy of the Manse in Polmuir Road in June 1982. Ian was to be the congregation's twelfth minister, but the first to be ordained and inducted. All his predecessors arrived at Ferryhill having already held a charge elsewhere. He was also the first to have entered the ministry as a second career - his first degree

Ferryhill South Woman's Guild Jubilee 1983. Presentation of pulpit fall created by Ruth Lough (4th right).

was in geography and he had held academic posts at the Universities of Edinburgh and Queensland.

JUBILEE

AT the beginning of his second year in Aberdeen, Ian found himself involved in the Jubilee Celebrations of the Ferryhill South Branch of the Woman's Guild. No question arose regarding the accuracy of the date on this occasion because it was well documented that the branch was founded in 1933 with the then Lady of the Manse, Mrs Stewart as the first President. One of the founding members was Margaret Iverach, daughter of the first minister. She subsequently served as President for several years. To mark the 50th anniversary the branch commissioned the well known local artist Ruth Lough to create a new pulpit fall and bible markers for use in the sanctuary.

By the early 1980s the health of Peter Davidson was beginning to give concern. After a series of absences, Parkinson's Disease was diagnosed. He had resigned as Presbytery Clerk but continued to do his best to meet the pastoral demands of the Ferryhill North congregation until 1984 when he announced his retirement. Once more, the question of Union was raised by the Presbytery Committee. This time the matter proceeded as far as the production of a draft basis of union. The Ferryhill South congregation consented, but a meeting of the Ferryhill North congregation voted against the proposal. Presbytery accepted the situation, but only to the extent that they granted Ferryhill North permission to appoint a minister on terminable tenure, and instructed both congregations to work towards achieving a union in five years. On that basis the Revd Andrew Christie moved from the linked charge of Clatt and Rhynie in October 1984. He was no stranger to Aberdeen, having been a "Co-op" grocer for some years and having acted as Sunday School Superintendent at the South Church. It was a famous minister of the South Church, Revd James Wood, who persuaded Andrew to study for the ministry. Two members of the Christie family suffered from disabling illness, making 26 Polmuir Road unsuitable as the Manse. It was sold and a modern house at 50 Sycamore Place was purchased.

THE ORGAN TRANSPLANT

VISITORS to Skibo Castle may find that Andrew Carnegie's pipe organ is still in existence. If so it has done rather better than its close relative which was installed in Ferryhill Free Church in 1903. By the end of 1986 an expert assessment of the instrument indicated that it was reaching the end of its working life. It had cost £1000 and was to serve for a few years yet, so the annual cost was approximately £11 - pretty good value. Rather than embark on a programme of restoration which would have cost in excess of £30,000 it was decided to open an Organ Fund with a view to purchasing an Allen Digital Organ. A deputation from the Kirk Session attended a demonstration in Beechgrove Church and came back convinced that the Church should invest in the modern technology represented by the Allen instrument.

Jimmy Shearer was appointed to administer the fund. He devised a scheme of regular and covenanted giving which proved remarkably successful. When the time came for the replacement of the organ, the funds were in place and there was sufficient left over to purchase a superb Steinway grand piano offered for sale by a retired music teacher living in Forgue.

ANOTHER CENTENARY

INCREASINGLY the Church was becoming aware of the importance of making the wider community aware of the range of activities con ducted under its banner. Thus it was that Merricks Arnott's 1938 concept of holding a Church Exhibition was repeated in 1986 by Ian Dick and his team at Ferryhill South. A few months later, in May 1987, the Centenary of the 1st Aberdeen Company of the Boys Brigade was celebrated. A combined Open Night was held in the nearby Fairfield House Drill Hall. The Inspecting Officer was the Brigade President, Viscount Thurso. To mark the centenary, a committee of BB parents and friends presented a new audio system for use in the church. The Kirk Session recognised the occasion by establishing a fund to enable officers and boys of the company to attend courses and camps at distant locations in the UK and overseas.

UNION AT LAST

AS the end of the decade approached it became clear that the Presbytery was sticking to its guns as far as the future of the churches in Ferryhill was concerned. Andrew Christie had been appointed for five years. In fact his tenure on Ferryhill North lasted a little longer, but the Presbytery was not to be deflected from its intention to bring about a union. Meetings were held, the congregations were cited to attend the Presbytery and a Basis of Union was arrived at with remarkably little disagreement. The two most important elements were that Ian Dick would be the first minister of the United Charge and that a Panel of Arbiters, appointed by the General Assembly, would decide which building would be used as the new congregation's place of worship. The Arbiters duly arrived and, having visited both churches, announced that the Ferryhill South building would henceforth be the home of the new Ferryhill Parish Church. It had already been agreed that the Dick family would continue to live at 54 Polmuir Road, so the manse in Sycamore Place and, of course, the old Ferryhill North Church building were put up for sale. The Union of the two congregations was finalised at a Presbytery service held on 30th October 1990. Ian Dick was inducted as the first minister of the new charge of Ferryhill Parish Church.

A FRESH START

FERRYHILL North and Ferryhill South both ceased to exist at the moment of Union. The minister and office-bearers went out of their way to make the congregation feel that this was a fresh start for everyone. The concept that "this is the way we do it" was ruled out of order. As a brand new congregation there were no traditions and no assumptions. For each component of congregational life the question was "How shall we deal with this?" New structures were put in place for running the congregation's affairs. The training of elders and office-bearers was introduced. The old system of elders' districts was discontinued. In its place Area Care Teams were created, involving other members along with elders in providing for the pastoral needs of the congregations. Instead of leaving everything to activists on the Kirk Session and Board, members were invited to join Task Groups, each of which was responsible for a particular aspect of the congregation's life and ministry. In this way the talents and interests of people could be made to match the responsibilities of the tasks they were given. The new system did not bring about a magical transformation, but it was based on common sense and spread responsibilities over a wider base so that more people could be involved.

Revd Ian Dick

OUTREACH AND WORSHIP

OUTREACH continued to be a priority. The services at residential homes continued, an annual social afternoon for the housebound and disabled was introduced, and a Summer Club for primary school children became a highlight of the year's programme.

No longer was the conduct of Sunday services left wholly to the Minister. Members of the congregation were encouraged to undertake scripture readings, and to lead the Call to Worship. The use of responses in prayers became a regular feature, as did the Gathering Song which preceded the call to Worship. Instead of having a regular church choir on duty at all services, the Ferryhill Singers were formed to rehearse musical items for Christmas, Easter and other special soccasions. During the summer holiday months, members of the congregation, working in groups, took responsibility for the conduct of entire services, usually with special themes. New life was breathed into congregational praise with the introduction of modern song collections, Sing Praise, Songs of God's People and Common Ground. On several occasions groups from the congregation visited Carberry and Iona, absorbing many ideas for enriching worship.

Modifications were made to the way in which the Sacrament of Communion was dispensed. The common cup was re-introduced for informal evening communion services. On some occasions communicants were invited to come forward and stand round the communion table to receive the Sacrament.

HERITAGE

AT the same time it was necessary to preserve as much as possible of the joint heritage of the two former churches. Communion table, chairs, font and lectern were carefully transported from the North Church and placed in the chancel of the new parish church. Jennifer Jane Bayliss, a stained glass specialist with studios in Fintray, was commissioned to design a trefoil "Window of Unity" to surmount the main entrance to the church. She was also consulted about the North Church windows, and in due course the Watson Nativity Window and the Wright memorial windows were installed in the new church. The Nativity Window formed the centre piece of the Sanctuary following an extensive programme of refurbishment and re-ordering that was set in hand soon after the Union.

TOWARDS 2000

USING funds from the sale of the redundant buildings, this formed the first part of a major development programme which was given the title "Ferryhill Towards 2000". Oliver Humphries, a distinguished local architect with offices in Albury Road, was invited to produce plans in which the main features were the clearing of the central chancel area and the partial removal of the side galleries. The aims of the Ferryhill South Organ Fund were now implemented by substituting an Allen Digital Organ for the old pipe organ. The cutting back of the galleries was a triumph of craftsmanship and made it possible for the east transept of the church to become a Memorial Chapel, accommodating memorial tablets, including war memorials, from both the former congregations. The Chapel was furnished with chairs, donated by members of the congregation, in many cases as memorials of loved ones.

With the side galleries reduced, windows which had been almost totally masked were revealed. One of these caught the attention of Jane Bayliss. She offered to donate a new stained glass window as a memorial to the 167 men who had lost their lives in the Piper Alpha Disaster which occurred on 6th July 1988. At that time a memorial service was held in Ferryhill South Church at the request of the Occidental Petroleum Company. Jane, whose husband was employed by Occidental, attended that service and was profoundly moved by it. The Piper Alpha Window, beside the east door, was dedicated on 25th October 1994 by the Moderator of the General Assembly, the Right Reverend James Simpson.

The window at the other side of the door was made available for a memorial to Archie and Joan Steele, stalwarts of the Kirk who had served as Session Clerk and President of the Woman's Guild respectively. A donation from their family made it possible to offer a further commission to Jane Bayliss to create a window that would balance the Piper Alpha Window and highlight important aspects of the Steele's lives. Jane produced a striking design based on the Genesis account of the Garden of Eden. The new window was dedicated in 1999. The changes to the Sanctuary were greatly admired and would undoubtedly have given satisfaction to the original architect of the building, Duncan McMillan. As we have seen, he was bitterly opposed to the siting of the organ pipe box and to the creation of the side galleries. The disappearance of the former and the substantial reduction of the latter would have met with his wholehearted approval.

MORE DEVELOPMENTS

THESE alterations, carried out during 1993-94 formed the first phase of the "Ferryhill Towards 2000" development programme designed to up-date the church building to fit it for congregational and community use in the third millennium. From the members' point of view it

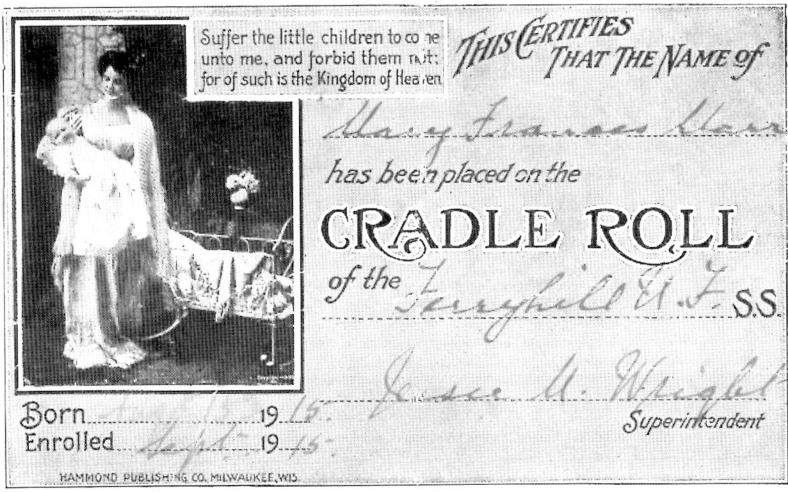

Mary Marr's Cradle Roll Certificate 1915

was a relatively painless operation, because funds were in hand following the sale of properties. The second phase involved creating new entrance and reception areas for the church and halls, providing a new kitchen and church office, and generally preparing the way for the church to be open and used seven days a week. This time the money had to be found. An appeal was launched and over several years all sorts of fund-raising projects were undertaken. Grants and loans were received from various quarters and eventually work on Phase Two began in the autumn of 1999. By Easter 2000, the transformation was almost complete and the new fellowship areas came into use. On Sunday 4th June, the new facilities were officially opened by Anne Begg MP and dedicated by the Moderator of Aberdeen Presbytery, the Revd Fred Coutts. Coinciding with the creation of these splendid new spaces came the reactivation of the Church Bell which had lain silent for many years. It was brought back to useful life by the installation of an electro-mechanical device, donated by the Community Council to mark the Millennium. The bell was rung by this method for the first time during a service attended by pupils of Ferryhill School. The switch was pressed by Mary Marr, one of the kirk's longest-serving office-bearers.

Within a few weeks of the official opening, the new Foyer came into service as a coffee shop on weekday mornings. The church office was moved from the basement to its new location in the tower, releasing space for the creation of an Archive Room, open to the public and containing memorabilia accumulated over the previous 127 years. The congregation took another step forward in July with the launch of its own web-site on the Internet.

AND NOW . . .

WITH 127 years of history behind them, mostly on two sites, the people of Ferryhill Parish Church entered the 21st Century occupying the prime geographical position that William Henderson and others first identified in 1873. The exterior of the building remained as a tribute to the vision of Duncan McMillan and the craftsmen he employed. Ferryhill itself retained much of the character of a Victorian suburb. Many of the fine 19th Century houses and tenements survived, and on the whole the 20th Century developments had fallen into place in a natural way that avoided the imposition of any artificial divisions in the community. Gap sites, such as those at Prince Charles Barracks and near the railway, continued to be filled by the housebuilders. This, plus an extension of the parish boundaries to take in part of the former Langstane parish, produced a significant increase in population as the new century arrived. In 2000 the construction of headquarters for the Talisman oil company in Holburn Street created a new landmark for Ferryhill and raised the commercial profile of the parish.

Environmentally, the Duthie Park is the jewel in Ferryhill's crown - representing the happiest possible marriage of private generosity and municipal foresight. With its school, library, post office, hotels, hostelries and shops, Ferryhill has all the characteristics of a village in the city. At its highest point and at its heart stands the Parish Church, now completing 126 years of service and standing ready to serve Christ and the Community in the new millennium. Perhaps it is neither immodest nor far-fetched to apply God's prophecy, as reported by Ezekiel, to Ferryhill: "*I will cause my people and their homes around my holy hill to be a blessing. And I will send showers, showers of blessings, which will come just when they are needed.*"

The Atrium – part of the new accommodation at Ferryhill Parish Church opened in May 2000.

September 2000 – construction work in progress at the Talisman building in Holburn Street, destined to be a major Ferryhill landmark.

BIBLIOGRAPHY

Apart from the records and congregational magazines of the Ferryhill Churches, the sources of information on which I have drawn include the following:

PJ Anderson, *Record of the Quatercentenary,* Aberdeen University Studies No. 29, 1906

William Carnie, *Reporting Reminiscences*, AUP, 1902, 1904, 1906

Revd Peter Davidson, *Ferryhill North Memories,* Privately Published, 1993

The Duthie Park, A Descriptive and Historical Sketch, Aberdeen Free Press, 1883

GM Fraser, *Aberdeen Street Names,* James G Bisset, 1986

Alexander Gammie, *The Churches of Aberdeen,* Aberdeen Daily Journal, 1909

James C Gilchrist, *Ferryhill South Church 100 Years,* Aberdeen Journals, 1974

Alexander Keith, *A Thousand Years of Aberdeen,* AUP, 1972

Hugh Mackenzie, *The City of Aberdeen,* Oliver and Boyd, 1953

Diane Morgan, *The Story of Ferryhill,* Leopard Magazine, 1977

Post Office Aberdeen Directory 1870 onwards

John Smith & David Stevenson (eds) *Aberdeen in the 19th Century,* AUP, 1988

Revd Robert Stewart, *Diamond Jubilee Retrospect,* Privately Published, 1934

Michael Thomson, *Silver Screen in the Silver City,* AUP, 1988

Fenton Wyness, *City by the Grey North Sea,* Alex P Reid & Sons, 1966